TEN TRUE TALES

HEROES
of 9/11

Allan Zullo

SCHOLASTIC INC.

New York   Toronto   London   Auckland
Sydney   Mexico City   New Delhi   Hong Kong

*To first-responders who risk their lives every day
to keep the rest of us safe.*
—A.Z.

ISBN 978-0-545-25506-6

12 11   14 15 16/0

Printed in the U.S.A.   40
First Scholastic printing, September 2011

Acknowledgments

I wish to thank the first-responders featured in this book for their willingness to relive in personal interviews with me the dramatic and sometimes emotional memories of their heroic exploits.

I am also grateful to Steve Ritea of the Fire Department of New York's public affairs office for his assistance.

Author's Note

The first-responders on September 11, 2001—firefighters, police officers, emergency medical technicians, and paramedics—as well as military officers and even many civilians risked their lives to save people they didn't know.

Every one of them is a hero. I wish I could write about all their personal stories of valor, honor, and sacrifice. Instead, I have written ten stories that reflect the countless breathtaking acts of heroism that occurred inside the World Trade Center, the Pentagon, and a hijacked plane.

For this book, I read hundreds of news accounts and transcriptions of radio transmissions, phone messages, e-mails, and oral histories from rescuers. Selecting a representative sample of these courageous people, I conducted personal, lengthy interviews and asked each to relive the heart-stopping moments when they risked their lives to save others. Some found it easy to recall their experiences. Some found it difficult and emotional because one or more of their comrades had been killed.

All persons profiled in this book shared a common trait—humility. None viewed themselves as heroes. Some said they were just doing the job they were trained to do while others said they were just doing the right thing. All said that the real heroes were the brave first-responders who sacrificed their lives in their valiant attempts to rescue others, the courageous everyday citizens who died trying to save coworkers, and the passengers and crew of a hijacked plane who thwarted the deadly mission of the terrorists on board.

As paramedic Charles Sereika told me, "All the real heroes died that day. The rest of us just did what we could."

By their actions, the heroes of 9/11 gave us a window into the human heart. Because they were committed to the service of their fellow man, they were willing to face death and take dangerous chances in their single-minded goal of saving others.

The triumphs of these brave heroes should be recognized not only by those whose lives were spared, but also by all of us. Their examples can offer us motivation to become the heroes of our own life story, of doing what's right no matter the risk. Each of us possesses an inner strength that is often left untouched. But it's ready to be

Author's Note

tapped—if we so choose—when we face a family crisis, an extraordinary circumstance, a perilous situation, a moral dilemma. That's how heroes are made.

The heroes of 9/11 mined their personal inner strengths. When you read the gripping accounts of their gutsy actions, you'll see that they displayed an intense boldness that spurred them to reach far beyond their personal limits.

Their stories are written as factual and truthful versions of their recollections, although some of the dialogue has been re-created.

This book is a salute to those who put their lives on the line every day—firefighters, police officers, and members of our armed forces—as well as to those who are called on by fate to risk everything for a greater good.

—A.Z.

Contents

ATTACK ON AMERICA

On September 11, 2001, the United States—and the world—changed forever.

In the bloodiest day on American soil since the Civil War, 19 members of the radical Islamic terrorist organization al-Qaeda hijacked four commercial jetliners and turned them into weapons of death and destruction.

At 8:46 A.M., American Airlines Flight 11 was deliberately crashed into the 110-story North Tower of the World Trade Center (WTC) in New York City. Seventeen minutes later, at 9:03 A.M., United Airlines Flight 175 plowed into the twin South Tower.

At 9:37 A.M., American Airlines Flight 77 smashed into the Pentagon, the nation's military headquarters near Washington, D.C. A fourth hijacked jet, United Airlines Flight 93, was aiming for the U.S. Capitol or the White House. But the courageous passengers and crew rebelled. At 10:02 A.M., during their desperate attempt to overpower the terrorists, the plane crashed in Pennsylvania, 20 minutes short of its intended target.

By the end of the day, 2,995 people were dead . . . and the world was in shock.

The plot to attack America was hatched by radical Muslim Khalid Sheikh Mohammed of Kuwait. It was approved by al-Qaeda's leader, Osama bin Laden, whose terrorist organization was based in Afghanistan. Their hatred for the United States was—and still is—fueled by their opposition to America's foreign policies. Under Mohammed's guidance, 19 young Muslim fundamentalists spent two years training for the deadly mission. Many of them had visas allowing them to live in the United States and take flying lessons.

Armed with smuggled knives and box cutters, the hijackers looked like ordinary passengers as they boarded the four jetliners. Once the planes were airborne, the terrorists took control of the aircrafts in coordinated suicide assaults. They chose coast-to-coast flights because those planes carried large amounts of fuel and would cause the biggest explosions on impact.

The enemy targeted the Twin Towers at the World Trade Center in New York's Financial District because the structures were mighty symbols of commerce. An estimated 14,000 workers were in the towers when they were attacked.

The first plane crashed into the north side of the

North Tower (1 WTC) between the ninety-third and ninety-ninth floors, setting the upper floors ablaze. Thousands of workers—including victims suffering from serious burns—began making an orderly evacuation down the building's three stairways. At impact, however, most of the tower's 99 elevators were rendered useless, trapping hundreds of people.

Meanwhile, people in the South Tower (2 WTC) began leaving. At first, most everyone assumed that this was a horrible accident. But then the second plane struck the South Tower between the seventy-seventh and eighty-fifth floors, igniting another colossal high-rise fire. That's when everyone realized the United States was under attack.

Office equipment, glass, and people were sucked out the windows and rained down on the streets below along with parts of planes and other debris. An estimated 600 people were on the floors where the planes struck, and were likely killed instantly. At least 1,500 workers survived the crashes, but were unable to escape the buildings because they were trapped above the impact areas. As the fires raged with no hope of rescue, an estimated 200 people leaped to their deaths rather than die from the flames.

Thousands of firefighters and 200 units—half the Fire Department of New York City (FDNY)—and thousands of officers from the New York Police Department (NYPD) as well as off-duty first-responders sped to the chaotic scene. Firefighters—

many wearing more than 100 pounds of gear—and other rescuers rushed into the burning towers. They began the torturous climb up the stairs of New York's two tallest buildings, boldly trying to save anyone they could. Thousands were helped out safely.

But the steel girders holding each floor began to soften from the heat of the flaming jet fuel until they could no longer bear the load. At 9:59 A.M., after burning for 56 minutes, the South Tower collapsed. Twenty-nine minutes later, the North Tower came crashing down. The astonishing life-crushing, earth-shaking collapses killed almost everyone still inside—workers and rescuers. Massive, powerful clouds of choking dust and pelting debris roared through the streets, engulfing thousands of people who had already fled the towers.

The falling rubble destroyed or seriously damaged other buildings in the complex. The nearby 47-story office building 7 WTC caught fire and collapsed later that afternoon at 5:21 P.M.

Miraculously, 20 people trapped inside the WTC buildings were rescued after the collapses. But the WTC attacks claimed the lives of 2,605 people (not including those on board the aircraft). Among the casualties: 411 heroic first-responders who were still trying to rescue people when the towers came down. The FDNY lost 343 members, the most of any fire department in the history of firefighting. The Port Authority Police Department suffered the greatest single-day loss of life in law enforcement history when 37 officers from every rank were killed. The NYPD bore law enforcement's second-worst death toll that day with 23 casualties. An additional eight emergency medical technicians (EMTs) and paramedics from private emergency medical services units also died.

While the Twin Towers were burning, the third hijacked plane swooped down and crashed into the west side of the Pentagon in Washington, D.C. The impact killed 125 persons, including 55 military personnel, and caused a fierce fire that caved in a wedge of the enormous building.

After United Flight 93 was hijacked over western Pennsylvania, the passengers and crew learned from onboard phone calls to loved ones about the WTC and Pentagon attacks. Knowing the terrorists on board were on a suicide mission to destroy another national landmark, the captives rose up against them in a spontaneous rebellion that ended when the jetliner crashed in a field near Shanksville, Pennsylvania. Like the three earlier hijacked planes, no one survived. The four doomed flights claimed the lives of 246 passengers and crewmembers in addition to the 19 terrorists.

Fearing more assaults, officials immediately shut down New York City's bridges, tunnels, and airports as well as museums and major skyscrapers like the Empire State Building. Then the order went nationwide. The Sears Tower in Chicago was evacuated, as were colleges and museums. Disney World shut down, Major League Baseball canceled its games, and nuclear power plants went to top-security status. The thousands of commercial and private planes that were still in the air were ordered to land at the nearest airport.

The United States quickly determined that the perpetrators were from al-Qaeda. Leader Osama bin Laden and his fellow fanatics were based in Afghanistan, where they had set up a network of camps to train radicals to carry out terrorism in other parts of the world. That country was under the control of the Taliban, a fundamentalist Islamic militia that had seized power in 1996. The Taliban granted al-Qaeda protection in Afghanistan's desolate mountains.

Nine days after the 9/11 attacks, the United States demanded that the Taliban turn over to the U.S. all the leaders of al-Qaeda, immediately close every terrorist training camp, and round up all of Afghanistan's terrorists and their supporters. The Taliban refused.

So on October 7, 2001, the United States and several allies (called coalition forces) launched Operation Enduring Freedom and invaded Afghanistan. Within three months, coalition forces — spearheaded by the U.S. Army, Navy, Air Force, and Marines — toppled the Taliban government, destroyed al-Qaeda training camps, and drove most of the militants into the Hindu Kush mountains bordering Pakistan. Khalid Sheikh Mohammed was captured in 2003 and, as of early 2011, awaits trial on nearly 3,000 murder charges. Although many of al-Qaeda's top leaders were killed or captured during this time, Osama bin Laden managed to escape and, from a secret location, urged terrorists around the world to attack western countries.

The United States has been battling the Taliban and al-Qaeda sympathizers in Afghanistan ever since the invasion. It has turned into the longest shooting war in American history.

On May 1, 2011—nearly ten years after the attacks—an elite U.S. counterterrorism team of Navy SEALs stormed a heavily fortified compound near Islamabad, Pakistan, and killed bin Laden, the most wanted man in the world. The team swooped into the compound in a daring nightime helicopter raid, triggering a fierce 40-minute firefight that ended in bin Laden's death. The troops identified his body and then buried him at sea.

Since September 11, 2001, life has changed but goes on. Security at airports and at public and private buildings and events has tightened considerably because of the 9/11 attacks.

At the WTC site, which became known as Ground Zero after the attack, the process of cleaning up the rubble and recovering human remains and personal items went on 24 hours a day, seven days a week, for eight months. A new WTC complex is now under construction. In 2006, a sleek 52-story office building was completed where 7 WTC once stood. Scheduled for completion in 2013 is the 102-story 1 WTC, which will soar to 1,776 feet—a height chosen to honor the year of America's independence. It will be about 400 feet taller than the

Twin Towers. Several other buildings are being constructed, including the National September 11 Memorial and Museum.

The damage to the Pentagon was cleared and repaired within a year of the attacks. The remodeled wedge contains the America's Heroes Memorial and a chapel at the spot where Flight 77 crashed into the building. Erected next to the Pentagon is a permanent outdoor memorial to the 184 people killed in the building and on the plane (not including the five hijackers).

Near Shanksville, Pennsylvania, the Flight 93 National Memorial park and tribute center opened its doors in 2011 on the tenth anniversary of the attacks.

September 11, 2001, will forever be etched in the souls of Americans. It was a day bloodied by terror and tragedy. But it was also a day of courage and character. The minutes and hours immediately after the horrifying attacks saw unbelievable acts of bravery by first-responders and ordinary citizens who rushed into harm's way to save countless lives.

In one of history's most inhuman moments, it is the humanity of heroes that will forever be remembered.

THE WORLD TRADE CENTER

The original World Trade Center (WTC) was a complex of seven buildings located in the heart of New York City's Financial District in lower Manhattan. Soaring above the site were two majestic 110-story office buildings, known as the Twin Towers.

Construction of the North Tower (1 WTC) was completed in December 1970, seven months before the completion of the South Tower (2 WTC). Connecting the two towers was the 22-story Marriott World Trade Center (3 WTC). Surrounding the towers were office buildings; the nine-story 4 WTC and 5 WTC; the eight-story 6 WTC, which housed the offices of the United States Customs and the United States Bureau of Alcohol, Tobacco and Firearms, among other government agencies; and the 47-story 7 WTC. Altogether, the main

World Trade Center complex, which was operated by the Port Authority of New York and New Jersey, covered 16 acres, large enough to have two zip codes and its own 1,333-person police department.

The towers were so tall that on a clear day, you could see for 45 miles from the observation deck. The buildings had 16 miles of staircases and 43,600 windows. Sixty-eight miles of steel were used in their construction and enough concrete to build a road from New York City to Washington, D.C.

More than 500 companies had offices in the Twin Towers. On a typical weekday, 50,000 people worked in the towers with another 100,000 passing through as visitors. An estimated 14,000 people were in the towers on the morning of September 11.

In the 17-minute period between the attack on the North Tower and the one on the South Tower, New York City and the Port Authority had mobilized the largest rescue operation in the city's history, with more than 1,000 first-responders, a number that would grow as the crisis worsened. Their main mission: save lives.

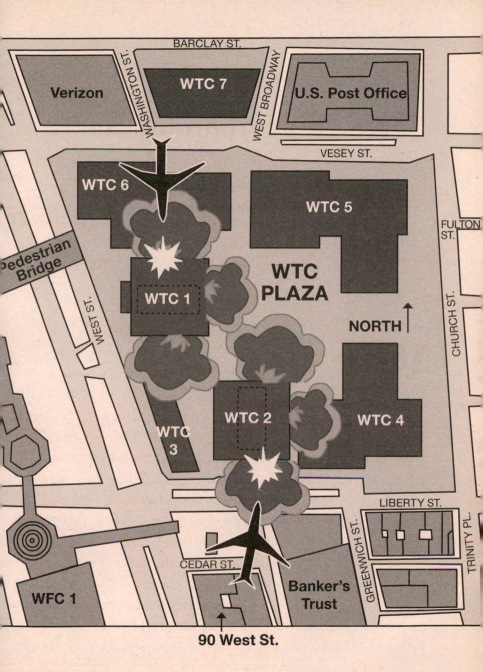

"We Can't Abandon Her"

CAPTAIN JOHN "JAY" JONAS
Fire Department of New York

World Trade Center . . . ten-sixty. Send every available ambulance, everything you've got to the World Trade Center . . . Now!"

In his 20-plus years at the Fire Department of New York, Captain Jay Jonas had never heard such a radio transmission before. "Ten-sixty" meant a catastrophic event. He and his five men from Chinatown's Ladder Company 6—nicknamed the Dragon Fighters—leaped onto their 50-foot-long hook-and-ladder truck, which then roared out of the firehouse. Mike "Mickey" Meldrum was behind the wheel while Matt Komorowski sat high on the truck's tail to steer the back end. Sal D'Agostino, Tommy Falco, and Billy Butler were in the back of the cab preparing themselves for a long day. In less than three minutes the bright red truck, which sported shiny brass dragons on its doors, covered the mile-and-a-half run.

From the shotgun seat, Jonas got his first look at the stricken North Tower. Smoke and flames were spewing out of gaping holes bored by American Airlines' Boeing 767 that had crashed between the ninety-third and ninety-ninth floors on the north face of the 110-story building.

Jonas, 43, who wrote the FDNY training manual for rescuing firefighters from high-rise fires, knew that each floor was roughly an acre. With the top 20 floors engulfed in flames, he was staring at a 20-acre fire raging 90 stories above. He thought, *This is the most unbelievable sight I've ever seen.*

It would soon become even more unbelievable.

After Meldrum weaved the rig through a current of fleeing people, he parked the truck on West Street in front of the North Tower (1 WTC). As the men began taking equipment off the vehicle, they were bombarded by falling fragments of office furniture, glass shards, chunks of the building, and parts of the jetliner.

"Run!" Jonas shouted.

The men took cover under the pedestrian bridge that spanned the four lanes of West Street and connected the North Tower to the World Financial Center. To retrieve their gear, Jonas kept watch until he could see a letup in the rain of debris. When it seemed clear, they dashed to the fire truck, grabbed their tools, and sprinted under the bridge. They darted back and forth three times to get what they needed. Then, lugging their gear, they hustled into the entrance of the burning building. It had been only ten minutes since the plane had slammed into 1 WTC.

Jonas and his men rushed into the shattered lobby where victims who had been burned in elevators were being treated. The firefighters reached the command post, a big console-like counter full of phones and monitors that were connected to smoke detectors and emergency communications throughout the building. Battalion Chief Joe Pfeifer and Deputy Fire Chief Peter Hayden were juggling several phones at once while barking orders to the growing number of firefighters who had arrived. Office workers by the hundreds streamed from the stairwells in surprisingly orderly columns and were ushered safely out.

Suddenly, the firefighters heard a loud explosion that shook the building. They rushed to the blown-out lobby windows and saw large pieces of falling metal and flaming debris slam into the ground. *Maybe a fuel tank on the plane blew up,* Jonas thought. Seconds later, a man in a business suit rushed in from outside and yelled, "A second plane just hit the other tower!"

"They're trying to kill us," Jonas declared. For several seconds, an eerie silence crept over the lobby.

A firefighter muttered to Jonas, "We're going to be lucky if we survive this."

Jonas nodded and said, "Good luck." When it was Jonas's turn to get orders, Hayden told him, "Just go upstairs and do the best you can."

"All right, Chief. You got it."

"We Can't Abandon Her"

Jonas hurried over to his men and said, "Okay. Here's the deal. We're going upstairs on a rescue mission to help out whoever needs it. The bad part is we can't take the elevators. After seeing those people burned coming out of the elevator, it's an unacceptable risk. That means we have to walk up ninety floors. We'll do ten floors at a time, take a quick breather, and push on for ten more so we'll have something left when we make it up there. I know walking up is a raw deal, but this is what we're doing."

Without hesitation they all said, "Okay, Cap, let's go. We're with you." No one had to tell them that in a high-rise, search-and-rescue teams always work as a unit, not as individuals. Whatever they would do, the six would do together.

The men were clad in leather boots with steel shanks, bunker pants, a life-saving harness, fire-retardant coat, gloves, hood, and leather helmet. They had flashlights, radios, air packs, coils of rope, rescue webbing, a six-foot hook, and a Halligan, which is like a crowbar with special edges. As typical members of a ladder company, Jonas's men each were carrying anywhere from 90 to 110 pounds of gear.

Although the two towers were among the tallest in the world, they each had only three stairwells—A, B, and C. One by one, the six men of Ladder 6 entered B, an average-sized lighted stairway at the center of the building's core. It had just enough room for the firefighters to walk up single file on the right while sweaty people pounded down the steps on the left. In the hot, stale air, the firefighters' bodies quickly heated up from exertion and from their bunker gear, which didn't allow the perspiration to evaporate and cool them down.

Water trickled down the lower stairs from burst pipes and sprinklers. The higher the firefighters climbed, the stronger the smell of jet fuel and smoke. And the building began creaking, cracking, and moaning.

As Jonas and his men slowly worked their way up, he was struck by how calm the civilians were. Many passing office workers patted the men and said, "God bless you," "Be careful," and "Thank you." Some smashed the glass fronts of the vending machines that were on each floor, pulled out bottles of water, and handed them to the firefighters.

One man lifted Tommy Falco's helmet and poured water over his head to cool him down.

Above the tenth floor, Jonas started seeing more victims. People suffering from severe lacerations and burns hobbled down the stairs with the help of coworkers. Men had taken off their suit jackets and covered up women whose clothes and skin had been burned off. *It's awful to see,* Jonas thought, *but this really is New York at its best. Everybody is doing the right thing, and they're doing it without being told.*

The firefighters also couldn't help but notice certain people like the angry man clutching a stuffed bunny while he was being carried down in a chair by Port Authority police officers; the overweight man strapped to a hand truck being wheeled down the stairs; or the blind man being led toward safety by his golden retriever.

Before making it to the twentieth floor, Jonas and his men had responded to two separate Mayday (distress-signal) messages. In both cases, a firefighter from another unit needed assistance because he was suffering from chest pains from the grueling climb. Once Jonas made sure each stricken man was getting medical assistance from EMTs, he and his crew pressed on, their legs straining and lungs burning.

When Jonas reached the twenty-seventh floor, he met Captain Billy Burke from Engine 21 and firefighter Andy Fredericks from Squad 18. Two of Jonas's men had become separated from the group after giving way to the people rushing down the stairs. While waiting for the pair, Jonas told the others, "Everybody take a knee and get some water. We'll take a quick break here and then head up to the fortieth on the next push."

Moments later, the men felt an earthquake-like shake and heard a loud rumbling noise. The building swayed back and forth, and then the lights went out for about 30 seconds. *What was that?* Jonas wondered. He turned to Burke and said, "Billy, you go check the windows on the south side, and I'll go check the windows on the north side. Maybe we can figure out what happened."

At the north windows, all Jonas could see was white swirling dust pressed against the glass. *Nothing could make that kind of dust except . . .* He met up with Burke back at the stairwell and said, "Billy, is that what I think it is?"

Burke nodded and said, "The South Tower just collapsed."

That was a difficult piece of information to process. In Jonas's entire career, no skyscraper had ever fallen down in New York. "I can't believe it," he murmured. He was fully aware that the North Tower was now in serious danger of collapsing, because the South Tower had toppled first even though it was attacked 17 minutes *after* the North Tower was struck. *My God, we're living on borrowed time.*

Jonas could no longer ignore the occasional groaning of the steel girders. Nor could he justify risking the lives of his men when a cave-in could happen at any moment. His heart said to keep going up, but his gut told him otherwise.

However, he hadn't received any evacuation orders from central command. Because radio communication was spotty at best, it was quite possible he hadn't heard such an order if it had been given. Looking up the stairwell, he didn't see any more civilians heading down. He knew that retreating without orders to do so meant he risked facing a reprimand by his superiors and humiliation from his fellow firefighters. Even so, he chose to follow his instinct. Jonas told his men, "It's time for us to leave."

It didn't feel right to the firefighters to abandon a burning building. But Jonas was firm. "If the South Tower can go, this one can go, too. We need to get out of here now."

Along with Burke and Fredericks, the men from

Ladder 6 turned around. D'Agostino asked if he could leave behind the 30-pound rescue rope he carried. "No, we will continue to bring everything," Jonas said for all to hear. "You never know what we're going to need on our way down."

Nearing the twentieth floor he heard on the radio an order for everybody to evacuate the North Tower. The message confirmed that he had made the right decision.

Two floors below, they spotted an older, heavy-set woman standing in the landing of the stairwell, whimpering in pain. Her name was Josephine Harris, a 59-year-old bookkeeper for the Port Authority. Even though she suffered from foot and leg problems, she had made it from the seventy-third floor down more than 50 stories with the help of coworkers. But when the South Tower fell, they had made the difficult decision to leave her and fled. Now Josephine had reached her physical limit and simply could go no farther.

"Cap, what do you want to do with her?" Tommy Falco asked.

"We can't leave her here. Bring her with us." Turning to Butler, considered the strongest man in the unit, Jonas said, "Billy, put her arm around your neck and guide her down the stairs."

At first she pleaded with them to go on without her. But they refused.

"Josephine, do you have kids?" Butler asked.

"Yes," she replied.

"And do you have grandkids?"

She nodded.

"Well, those kids want to see you again, so we have to get you out of this building, okay?"

Every man took a piece of Butler's gear to lighten his load. However, helping Josephine greatly slowed their descent. Before encountering her, they had been moving down at a fast clip. But now they were going at a snail's pace, creating a bottleneck for the first-responders behind them. The group repeatedly stepped aside to allow firefighters, police officers, and others to rush past them. Even though the men from Ladder 6 were anxious to get out of there, they remained together. They would live or die as a unit.

By the fifteenth floor, they had been joined by Lieutenant Mickey Kross from Engine 16 and by Rich Picciotto, a battalion chief who was using a bullhorn to order firefighters to evacuate immediately. Jonas soon spotted Faustino Apostol, Jr., aide to Second Battalion Chief William McGovern, standing in the doorway off the stairwell. "Faust, c'mon, let's go," Jonas urged. "It's time to leave. Come with us."

"It's okay, Cap. I'm waiting for the chief." No way was he going to abandon McGovern, who was somewhere else on the floor.

Jonas's radio began getting better reception. He heard a transmission from Captain Paddy Brown from Ladder 3 saying that he had several burned people on the fortieth floor, and he had no intention of leaving them behind.

"We Can't Abandon Her"

On the twelfth floor stairway landing, the group ran into members of Ladder Company 5 caring for an office worker who was having chest pains. Ladder 5's officer, Lieutenant Michael Warchola, was a good friend of Jonas's.

"Mike, c'mon," said Jonas. "It's time to go."

"I know, Jay, but we're still working on this guy," Warchola replied. Pointing to Josephine, he added, "You have your civilian, and I have mine. We'll be right behind you."

As Jonas and his group continued down ever so slowly, Captain Burke and Fredericks broke off to either hook up with their own units or help someone in need. Walking behind Butler and Josephine, Jonas calmly but firmly kept telling his men, "Let's go, fellas. Let's speed it up. Josephine, you can do it." In his head, though, he was screaming, "If we don't move faster, we're not going to make it!" His stomach was twisted in knots. Throughout his entire career as a lieutenant and a captain, he had never lost a man. Now all their lives were in jeopardy.

Josephine was growing weaker, and her legs were turning to jelly. On the fifth floor, Falco and Butler propped the woman up between them and half carried her. A tenth person had now joined the group—David Lim, a Port Authority police officer.

When they reached the fourth-floor landing, Jonas was starting to feel better about their chances. *Maybe this building won't fall down. Maybe we'll get out of here alive and everything will be okay.*

Just then, Josephine's legs gave way. She slumped to the concrete floor, crying, "Stop! Leave me alone. I can't go any farther."

This is bad, Jonas thought. *This is really bad.* His nerves on edge, he could almost hear the clock of doom ticking in his head. *Tick tock . . . We must keep moving . . . Tick tock . . . We can't abandon her . . . Tick tock . . . We need something to carry her in to take the weight off her feet. . . . Tick tock . . . I know, an office chair!*

With a special tool he always carried, Jonas snapped the lock of a fourth-floor door and frantically searched for a sturdy chair. Unfortunately, the group was on a floor that housed only mechanical and ventilation equipment, so he couldn't find a suitable chair. *This isn't working out. I've got to get back to the stairway and tell them we're just going to have to drag her down the steps.*

He ran toward the stairway door and was about four feet away when he felt an odd sensation. The floor he was standing on began vibrating and then rippled like a breeze-swept lake. *Is the building coming down?* He lunged for the door, but it wouldn't open. The entire North Tower was now twisting and shifting, preventing the door from opening. He yanked on the door again, and this time it opened.

Jonas dove for the landing as a sudden gust whooshed down the stairway at hurricane-force speeds. The blast of air picked up 190-pound Matt Komorowski, who was carrying 90 pounds of gear, and flung him like a rag doll down three flights. Also hurled down the steps were Chief Picciotto and Meldrum, the 6-foot-5-inch, 240-pound chauffeur of Ladder 6. D'Agostino was slammed against the wall, while Butler tumbled to the next landing.

As the stairway wobbled and swayed, Josephine lay on the floor covered by Lim and Falco, who had thrown their bodies over her. The rest of the fire-fighters crouched low and gripped the railing against the rush of air.

Before anyone had time to think, the stairway echoed with a frightening series of incredibly loud and rapid booms.

BANG . . . BANG . . . BANG . . . BANG . . . BANG . . .

They were experiencing a noise that nobody had ever heard before this day—the sound of a 110-story building falling down.

The floors were collapsing in pancake fashion. One floor would fall onto the next floor, which would give way onto the floor below, and so on all the way down. With each awful bang, everyone was thrown around the landing and steps as the compressive force from the collapsing floors above shoved air down the stairwell.

The sound grew louder and faster as the falling floors came closer and closer. Mixed into the din were the screeches of massive steel beams and girders twisting and bending. The earsplitting noise was like a hundred trains hitting their brakes at the same time, only more shrill.

We didn't make it, Jonas thought. *We came so close to getting out. It just wasn't enough. So this is how it ends.* Curled up in a ball and getting pelted by debris, he listened to the floors slamming onto one another and wondered how long he had left before being crushed to death.

After 13 horrifying seconds, the deafening bangs stopped and everything went silent. *I'm not dead! I'm not dead! Oh, man, I can't believe I survived this!*

In the dark, dust-filled stairway, Jonas, like everyone else, was coughing and gagging because it was so hard to breathe. With his fingers, he scraped thick powder, pulverized glass, and mashed sheetrock from his mouth, nose, eyes, and ears. When he gathered his wits, he took a roll call. To his great relief, everybody, including Josephine, who was still clutching her purse, answered, "Here."

It's a miracle! We're all alive!

The entire North Tower had collapsed except for one small section. Incredibly, the stairwell from basically the first-floor landing to the fifth floor—above and below the landing where Josephine Harris had flung herself to the floor—remained standing. The stairs between the second and third floor were missing, and so were sections of the landings. Because much of the stairwell was unstable, most everyone stayed put. They were concerned that moving the wrong way could set off a secondary collapse of their little area.

The survivors didn't understand that the whole building had fallen. Many assumed that, at worst, maybe half of the North Tower had come down. All they knew for sure was that they were alive . . . and trapped.

As the thick dust slowly settled, the survivors looked like ghosts shrouded in white grime that had powdered them from their hair to their shoes. Everyone was bruised, battered, and bleeding, but not seriously injured other than a concussion, bruised ribs, and a separated shoulder. *We're not in the greatest shape, but at least none of us have anything life threatening,* Jonas thought. Dust continued to clog their noses and mouths, and every time they blinked, it felt as though the insides of their eyelids were made of sandpaper.

Rich Picciotto had ended up on the third floor, Mickey Kross on the second, and Komorowski on the landing below him. Also on the second floor were Lieutenant Jim McGlynn and firefighter Bob Bacon from Engine 39. Minutes before the collapse, they and firefighters Jeff Coniglio and Jim Efthimiades had escorted several civilians out of the building. After doing a roll call, McGlynn had realized that fellow firefighter John Drumm was missing and last seen tending to a civilian on the second floor. So the four firefighters had dashed back into the North Tower and were looking for Drumm when the building came crashing down.

Efthimiades and Coniglio were now confined in a tiny space behind debris on the first-floor landing. They weren't hurt, but they yelled up that Battalion Chief Richard Prunty was pinned by an I-beam in the lobby and fading fast. They couldn't see him, but they could hear him so they knew he was close by. Komorowski's efforts to dig down to them were blocked by the rubble.

Meanwhile, Picciotto began broadcasting a Mayday over his radio, but wasn't getting any response.

When Jonas tried a different channel on his own radio, it came to life. He heard a heartbreaking message from a firefighter who was in obvious pain: "Just tell my wife and kids that I love them." Another transmission came from Warchola, the friend he passed on the twelfth floor landing. "Mayday! Mayday! Mayday! This is the officer of Ladder Company Five. I'm in Stairwell B on the twelfth floor. I'm trapped and I'm hurt bad."

Even though the stairway was missing steps, unstable, and strewn with debris, Jonas knew he had to try to save his buddy. Carefully, he climbed to the fifth floor only to reach a dead end. He couldn't move the rubble, because the chunks of concrete were too big and heavy.

Warchola sent out a second Mayday and then a third in a shaky voice that kept getting weaker as Jonas frantically searched for an opening. It was hopeless. He had to give up. His heart ripped with anguish, Jonas radioed his longtime friend, "I'm so sorry, Mike. I can't get to you."

No one knew it at the time, but there no longer was a twelfth floor. Warchola was actually trapped on the other side of the debris above the fifth floor. He never radioed again.

On the way back, Jonas found Picciotto's bullhorn and picked it up. *This could come in handy,* he thought.

Over the next hour, he stayed in radio contact with Chief Prunty. But every time they spoke, Jonas could hear him going deeper and deeper into shock. Jonas felt powerless. *It's so frustrating. There's nothing we can do for him.*

But there was something he could do for the survivors—find a way out. *We can possibly dust ourselves off and work our way down to the lobby or the basement and then maybe get out of the building.* But that plan was foiled when Komorowski, who was at the bottom of the stairs, yelled up, "Don't come down. There's no way out. It's packed with debris."

Falco asked Jonas, "Hey, Cap, what do we do now?"

"I don't know." Then, flashing a grin, he added, "I'm making this up as we go along."

Jonas started radioing Mayday messages on a different channel than the one Picciotto was using. It took 40 minutes, but eventually Jonas received a response. Deputy Chief Tom Haring radioed back, "Okay, Ladder Six. I have you recorded. You're in Stairwell B of the North Tower. We'll send people to get you out."

That makes me feel good. They know we're here. They know we're alive. Soon Jonas's radio crackled with more transmissions from searchers looking for the survivors. "Rescue Three to Ladder Six. Jay, this is Cliff," said friend, neighbor, and fellow firefighter Cliff Stabner. "I'm coming to get you, brother. I'm coming to get you."

Although most of those who radioed Jonas didn't mention how difficult it would be to find them, First Battalion Chief Bill Blaich told him, "It's really bad out here, Jay. It's going to take a long time for us to get to you, but I have the entire off-duty platoon of Ladder Eleven and Ladder Six with me."

Blaich's blunt assessment made Jonas think of the worst-case scenario. Using simple math—they were on the fourth floor of what had been a 110-story building—he figured that if the entire building had come down, they could be buried under 106 floors of debris. *Geez, it will definitely take a long time to get to us.*

"We just have to be patient," Jonas told the group. Everybody stayed quiet as they listened for rescuers. The silence was broken mainly by the hiss and crackle of fires breaking out nearby. Occasionally an explosion rattled their tomb.

After one blast that seemed much too close, Josephine whimpered, "I'm scared."

In the calmest voice he could muster, Jonas replied, "That's all right, darling. We're all a little scared. Just hang in there. We'll take good care of you." The men took turns comforting her.

Deputy Chief Nick Visconti radioed Jonas, "Operations Post to Ladder Six. Jay, where are you?"

Jonas gave precise directions to his location: Tower 1, Stairwell B, first to fifth floor. Over the next hour, he had to repeat his location again and again. He was getting discouraged. *What is taking them so long? This isn't that hard, gentlemen.* Jonas had no concept of what it looked like outside—a 16-acre landscape of twisted metal, truck-size chunks of concrete, and gaping holes licked by flames and smothered by smoke. With no landmarks, it was extremely challenging for the searchers to know where to start looking.

Then over the radio Jonas heard a firefighter ask, "Where's the North Tower?"

What do you mean "Where's the North Tower?" Jonas thought. *It's one of those big buildings on the corner. Oh, we're in trouble if they don't even know where the North Tower is.*

The search-and-rescue teams slowly treaded across the massive debris field. Every so often, Picciotto pushed a button on his bullhorn, emitting a siren that he hoped would help searchers pinpoint the location of the survivors.

Three hours had elapsed since they were trapped. Jonas was lost in thought when his eyes focused on a narrow beam of light that unexpectedly shined on the stairway. Others saw it, too. He jerked up and looked for the source. *It's the sun!*

The settling dust and angle of the sun had revealed a hole above and off to the side—a promising way out. It also indicated to them that the entire building had collapsed. "Guys, there used to be one hundred and six floors above us, and now I'm seeing sunshine!" Jonas said. "There's nothing above us. That big building we were in doesn't exist anymore."

As more light filtered in through gaps in the stairwell's shaft, Tommy Falco used his Halligan to widen the hole above the fourth-floor landing. He looked out and saw that the hole was about a dozen feet above the debris field, making it too far to jump. Jonas called for the rescue rope that he had refused to let D'Agostino leave behind during their evacuation. Butler tied one end to the stairway railing and the other to a harness on Picciotto, who wanted to be the first one out.

They needed to move cautiously. Picciotto exited the hole, slid down the rope, and tied it off. Carrying the bullhorn, he pressed the button that emitted a siren. Through the smoke, the siren caught the attention of the rescuers from Ladder 43.

One by one, Jonas sent people out of the tomb—Matt Komorowski, David Lim, Mickey Kross, Bob Bacon, Mike Meldrum, Billy Butler, and Sal D'Agostino. Jonas and Tommy Falco stayed behind with Josephine and waited for the men of Ladder 43 to take over Josephine's rescue. Jonas knew that he and the others were so battered and dehydrated that if they stayed much longer, they wouldn't be able to get themselves out, much less Josephine. She would have to be carried out on a special orange stretcher known as a Stokes basket.

Jim McGlynn, the lieutenant from Engine 39, chose to remain on the stairwell because two of his men were still trapped. "I'm not leaving without my guys," he insisted.

When Ladder 43's commander, Lieutenant Glenn Rohan, showed up, Jonas briefed him about Josephine, the two trapped firefighters, and Chief Prunty and Lieutenant Warchola.

Then Falco left the stairwell through the hole.

Seconds later, he turned around, poked his head back in, and told Jonas, "Hey, Cap, wait until you get a load of this."

When Jonas went out the hole, he gasped at the astonishing sight in front of him—the vast smoking debris field of bent steel and concrete chunks, all covered in gray. *I don't believe this! It looks like a nuclear bomb struck New York City.* A 14-story-high section of the façade (the front of the building) was all that was left standing from the North Tower. Trying to comprehend the total destruction, he thought, *I can't believe we survived this.* Across the way, flames were savaging three more buildings—5, 6, and 7 WTC.

The ordeal wasn't over for the survivors of Stairwell B. They still had to cross over the smoldering rubble and around the deadly voids. There was no solid footing and, even worse, the dust on the beams and metal made them as slick as ice.

When they neared 6 WTC, which housed regional offices of the CIA, FBI, and Secret Service, Jonas and his men heard gunfire. Ammunition, which had been stored in the offices, was exploding. *That's just great,* he thought. *All I need now is to be hit by some stray shot.* They were forced to change direction and try another route off the rubble.

Because the underground parking area and basement offices had collapsed, the survivors now faced a three-story-deep trench that they had to enter and climb back out of before they could reach safety. "Keep moving, keep moving," Jonas urged his men, some of whom were stumbling from sheer exhaustion. "We're not out of this yet."

Meldrum, who had suffered a concussion that made walking difficult for him, finally faltered. "Cap, I can't do it. I can't take another step."

"Yes you can, Mike. Just think about your wife and kids. You can do it. You have to do it."

Meldrum and the others trudged forward as Jonas continued to offer encouragement, as much for himself as for his men. When they finally reached the other side of the trench, they stared at a 30-foot-high hill—the final barrier between them and the end of their ordeal. Firefighters above dropped ropes to the weary survivors, who somehow mustered the strength to reach the top. Once he knew everyone was safe, Jonas made his climb. At the crest, a wave of relief swept over him. He always felt that his number one job was to make sure that all his men made it home alive at the end of each day.

Some of the survivors were immediately treated at the scene by EMTs, including Butler and Komorowski, who needed IVs because they were dehydrated. They were then transported to the hospital.

Before he would allow an EMT to examine him, Jonas headed over to the command post where Chief Hayden was shouting out orders from atop a fire department pumper to dozens of fresh firefighters arriving on the scene.

Above the din of chatter, engines, and heavy

machinery, Jonas stood next to the pumper and shouted, "Hey, Chief!"

At first, Hayden didn't hear him, so Jonas hollered several more times. Finally Hayden looked down and broke out in a big smile when he recognized the grime-covered, worn-out captain.

"We made it out!" Jonas said.

"Jay, it's good to see you," replied Hayden, his eyes welling up.

Jonas, who was teary eyed, too, straightened his back, snapped off a sharp salute, and said, "It's good to be here."

Nearby, the dust covered the wreckage of his hook-and-ladder truck, which had been crushed to its axles by the building's collapse. The only thing left of the truck's brass dragons was a snapped-off tail.

Word soon spread that the two trapped firefighters from Engine 39—Jeff Coniglio and Jim Efthimiades—had been freed and that Drumm had made it out before the collapse.

Jonas learned that Josephine had been brought out and taken to the hospital for observation. She would be fine.

Despite all that he had gone through, Jonas decided to walk the mile and a half back to the firehouse. On the way, he thought about Josephine. *If it hadn't been for her, there's a good chance we'd be dead right now.* Josephine had slowed them down just enough so that they were between the second and fifth floor when the building came down. Had they left her and run for their lives, they likely would have been killed. *By saving her, we unknowingly were saving ourselves.*

Five days after the attack, Jay Jonas was promoted to battalion chief. In 2007, he was named a deputy chief.

Many of the firefighters whom Jonas had met on the stairwell before the collapse or talked to on the radio afterward perished, including Chief Richard Prunty, Lieutenant Mike Warchola, Captain Billy Burke, Captain Paddy Brown, and firefighter Andy Fredericks.

More than 1,400 people died inside the North Tower when it fell. Only 14 survived—Jay Jonas and his group and the three firefighters from Engine 39. They were all trapped between the first and fifth floors of Stairwell B.

"We just happened to be in the right spot," says Jonas, after having time to reflect. "There was nothing magical about it. There was one pocket, one void, and we happened to be in it. When we got out, I assumed there were hundreds of pockets where people were safe but trapped. It took me about a week to realize that nobody else was coming out, and that was a shock.

"We lost about 2,800 people at the World Trade Center. But considering that 50,000 people worked in those buildings, the death toll, as hard as it is to accept, would have been much higher if it hadn't been for the efforts of the firefighters. The ones who sacrificed their lives are the real heroes."

"Get Everybody Out Now!"

OFFICER DAVID LIM
Port Authority Police Department

As office workers scrambled down the stuffy, crowded stairway of 1 WTC, Port Authority Police Officer David Lim was advancing up the steps with one thought in mind: *Get everybody out now!*

Seeing those heading in the opposite direction, he knew the situation was getting worse the higher he climbed. More people were bleeding. More were burned. More were scared.

Earlier that morning, Lim and his canine partner, Sirius, a specially trained bomb-sniffing yellow Labrador retriever, had been randomly checking for explosives in vehicles entering one of the WTC's service ramps. During their break, the K-9 team went to Lim's basement office underneath the South Tower. A veteran of 21 years on the force, Lim filled out paperwork while eating his usual breakfast of a bran muffin, banana, and coffee. At his feet, Sirius was devouring a bowl of dog food.

Lim liked to call Sirius "a big mush," because the four-year-old dog was so laid back. When on duty searching for explosives, Sirius—who wore Badge 17—remained alert, working long hours without signs of boredom or fatigue. But when his job was done, he couldn't wait to curl up and nap in his cage in the office. At home, though, Sirius was simply the loveable family pet who slept in Lim's bedroom.

At 8:46 A.M., a severe jolt shook Lim's office for several seconds. "What was that?" he asked Sirius. Seconds later, he heard over his radio that there had been an explosion on the upper floors of the North Tower. "Oh my God, Sirius, something got by us." Lim feared that a bomb-laden package from a delivery truck had cleared their checkpoint and been taken to an upper floor where it had detonated.

At the time, he wasn't aware that a jetliner had slammed into the tower. The impact had sparked a massive fire on the top floors and shot a fireball, fed by jet fuel, down a bank of elevators that flashed and burned on various levels all the way to the basement.

Because Sirius was a bomb dog and not a search-and-rescue dog, Lim left him in his cage. "You'll be safer here," Lim told him. "I'm going to help some people, but I'll come back for you later. I promise." Sirius looked up as if he understood. He then lay his head back down and watched his master charge out the door to assist in the evacuation.

From an early age, helping people was what Lim always wanted to do. Born and raised in New York City, Lim, a first-generation Chinese-American, was inspired to become a cop after developing a bond with the officers of the 101st Precinct in Queens. They often ate at his immigrant parents' restaurant in Far Rockaway, Queens, where he worked after school. In 1980, he joined the Port Authority Police Department (PAPD), which was responsible for the public safety of the entire WTC complex. On 9/11, members of the PAPD were the first of the first-responders.

After sprinting through the basement of the complex, Lim reached the plaza level of the North Tower. He saw hundreds of people—many of them women carrying their high-heel shoes—scrambling down the escalators and into the lobby.

While Lim was directing the flow of office workers out of the building, he heard a high-pitched scream. He wheeled around and saw on the plaza outside the remains of someone who had leaped from one of the upper floors. He dashed to the spot to investigate. Lim called his command desk and while he was reporting the incident, another jumper fell right in front of him. *If I had been ten feet closer, I would've been killed,* he thought.

Lim stared at the smoke belching from the top floors and told himself, *Things must be really bad up there for them to be jumping.* His heart ached for those people who felt so hopeless and desperate they were choosing to leap to their deaths rather than be burned alive. *I know I can do good here on the plaza helping evacuate people, but if others are thinking of jumping out of windows, they need my help upstairs.*

He had worked at the WTC for 16 of his 21 years on the force, and knew all its nooks and crannies. It was like a second home to him. Leaving the evacuation to an NYPD officer, Lim entered the crowded Stairwell A and started the strenuous climb toward the upper floors. He felt fortunate that he wasn't weighed down by all the gear and equipment that the firefighters carried. The only extra weight he had was a 15-pound gun belt. Adrenaline pumping through his 5-foot-7-inch, 175-pound frame spurred him up the steps.

During his climb, he heard over his radio that the explosion had been caused by a plane that had crashed into the building. He felt a sense of relief that it wasn't a bomb that had slipped by Sirius and him. Lim assumed that a small private plane had accidentally hit the North Tower.

Soon a radio transmission reported the plane that struck the building was a jetliner—and that the fire was spreading throughout the top 20 floors. The news hit him hard in the gut because first-responders like him were now dealing with an emergency no one had ever faced before. One concern he didn't have: that the tower would collapse. He knew the WTC structures were built to withstand a plane crash. Besides, he was at the scene in 1993 when terrorists tried but failed to bring down the North Tower. Back then, a powerful car bomb blew up in the underground garage, killing six and injuring more than 1,000 people, but the building still stood tall.

While heading up the stairway, Lim passed office workers who didn't know why they were being evacuated. Taking up both sides of the stairway, they were annoyed that they had to make room for Lim. "Why do we have to go down when you're going up?" someone asked him.

"Just keep going down," Lim said. "Down is good. It's a good thing."

"But why are you going up?"

"To tell people like you to keep going down."

Moments later, his radio transmitted an ominous message: "A plane has just hit Two World Trade Center!" Lim felt a surge of anxiety. *We're not dealing with an accident,* he thought. *We're under attack!* He lowered the volume on his radio so others in the stairway wouldn't hear it and panic.

When he exited Stairwell A on the twenty-seventh floor, Lim spotted a man in a wheelchair accompanied by a coworker. "Do you need my help?" Lim asked.

"No," the disabled man replied. "We're just waiting for the other people to go down first so we don't get in their way."

"You need to get out right now," Lim urged.

Seeing several firefighters who had emerged from

the doorway of Stairwell B, Lim told them about the man in the wheelchair. "Someone needs to help him get out of here," he told them.

"Don't worry," replied one of the firefighters. "We'll take care of him."

On the floor, Lim was stunned to see office workers still at their desks, unaware of the danger and waiting for official instructions. He ordered them to leave immediately. "Whatever you do, do not . . . I repeat, do not . . . take the elevators." He was afraid that the building's elevators could be death traps in the fire.

Figuring this might be his only chance for a break during the crisis, he used an office phone to call his wife, Diane. "I'm in the North Tower, but I want you to know that I'm okay," he told her. "I have to get as many people out of here as I can."

Rather than return to Stairwell A, he continued his climb via Stairwell B. Now he was seeing people who were dazed and bleeding; others whose skin and clothes were charred. Believing there were more victims farther up who needed his help, he began enlisting people who weren't hurt. He grabbed fit men by the arm and matched up each of them with someone who was injured or burned. In each case, he ordered, "Take this person all the way down and go straight to the triage area." (He was referring to a spot near the World Financial Center across the street where paramedics and EMTs were treating victims.) To speed up the evacuation of the injured, Lim told them to ignore the single-file line that was going down on the right, and instead go on the left against the traffic of the climbing cops and fire-fighters because they would step aside.

One man whom Lim had enlisted to escort a burn victim was hesitant about using the left side.

"I'll tell you what you do," said Lim. He looked down the stairway and bellowed, "Make way for the injured! Make way for the injured!" Turning to the man, he said, "Just shout that all the way down. Now go, go, go!"

Sweating and puffing, Lim arrived at the forty-fourth floor and hurried into the Sky Lobby. He unlocked the emergency closets, which stored gear such as axes, oxygen tanks, and flashlights. He handed out the equipment to several fatigued firefighters who had dropped their gear on the way up to lighten their load on the strenuous climb.

Suddenly, a thundering roar rocked the building. An unseen force blew out the south-facing windows and knocked down Lim and everyone around him. When he scrambled to his feet, he thought, *I don't know what just happened, but it must be bad. It feels like part of the building is collapsing. But, no, it can't be.*

"Everyone, listen up!" he ordered. "We have to get out of here right now!" He gathered the remaining office workers and herded them to Stairwell B. Despite the urgency, he was pleased to see that most everyone remained relatively calm and quiet as they hurried down the stairs. There was little panic and little talk.

The stairway's lights kept flickering, casting an eerie atmosphere on the emergency.

Then he heard a frightening message: "Tower Two is down! I repeat. Tower Two is down! All units, evacuate Tower One immediately!"

My God, the South Tower just fell! But that's impossible. This is the World Trade Center. Nothing can bring these buildings down. But the unbelievable had just happened. For the first time since the crisis began, Lim was genuinely scared. *This building will probably come down, too!*

As fast as he could, he helped clear each floor. Along the way, he and the firefighters were collecting the stragglers—those who were disabled, elderly, or overweight. Some of them deliberately were holding back so they wouldn't slow down the line. Lim would have none of that. "Everybody goes now!" he declared. "Nobody waits."

When he reached the twenty-seventh floor, Lim looked for the man in the wheelchair whom he had met on the way up. Lim was relieved he wasn't there. *He must have made it out.*

Around the twenty-first floor, he came across Chief James Romito, Captain Kathy Mazza, and Lieutenant Robert Cirri, all from the Port Authority Police Department. They were tending to a man who was having trouble breathing. Lim told the chief, "You know, the South Tower collapsed."

Romito grabbed his pager and read the message

confirming what Lim had just said. "Okay, let's get out of here." Romito and Cirri picked up the man under each arm and started down the stairs followed by Mazza and Lim.

The pace wasn't nearly as fast as Lim had hoped. *Time is limited and at this rate I'm probably not going to make it,* he fretted. *It's going to come down while I'm still in it.*

When they arrived at the fifth floor, Lim saw Port Authority employee Josephine Harris sitting on the side of the landing with several firefighters from Ladder 6 looking after her. People were stepping around her, including Romito, Mazza, and Cirri with their ill victim.

Lim learned that Josephine was too exhausted and in too much pain to go any farther. She just wanted to be left behind so the rest could get out quicker. But the firefighters refused.

One of the men told Lim that their captain, Jay Jonas, was on the fourth floor looking for a chair for her.

"There are no chairs on that floor," Lim said. "It's a mechanical and equipment room. Come on, I'll help you with Josephine." He lifted her by one arm while firefighter Tommy Falco took the other, and together they slowly headed down.

From a few landings below, Mazza called up to Lim, "Leave the woman with the firefighters and come with us."

"Go ahead, boss," he replied. "I'll be right behind you. I've already got her." It was the first time Lim had ever ignored a senior officer's command.

He made it down only one more floor before the building began shaking and rumbling so violently that it knocked everyone off their feet. The North Tower was beginning to collapse.

Lim and Falco covered Josephine with their bodies as the floors above fell one atop the other with increasing speed and intensity. Lim prepared himself for death. *I hope it's quick,* he told himself. *I don't want to be lying here trapped for days and then die.* The screeching, thundering din was unlike anything he had ever heard before. As the collapsing floors tumbled closer and closer, he pictured in his mind his wife, Diane, and children, Michael and Debra. He wanted the family to be his last thought on earth.

It was all over in 13 seconds. Lim and the others were now enveloped in a blanket of darkness, dust, and debris. And silence. At first he thought, *I must be dead.* Then he coughed. *Dead men don't cough.*

He couldn't see anyone because it was totally black. The dust was so thick that the only way he could breathe was by pulling his shirt over his face. Hacking away and fighting for a decent breath, Lim tried to gather his wits. *My God, I survived!*

Then Lim heard Captain Jonas call out, "Is everyone all right? Sound off!" One by one, Lim, Josephine, and a dozen firefighters who were sprawled from the fifth floor down to the first answered the roll call. Lim waited to hear the voices of Mazza, Romito, and Cirri. When he didn't, he hoped it was because they had fled the building in time.

Meanwhile, firefighter Mickey Meldrum had fallen on a landing between what was left of the third and fourth floors. He found himself stuck on a small foot-and-a-half-wide chunk of concrete, his legs dangling over a space where steps used to be. Now it just looked like a dark hole. Meldrum complained that he couldn't feel his arms or legs. He felt dizzy, his head hurt, and his speech was slurred.

He had the classic symptoms of a concussion. Firefighters tied a rope around Meldrum and attached it to a railing so he wouldn't slip off. To prevent him from losing consciousness or falling asleep—a medical concern for someone with a concussion—Lim kept talking to him, asking questions about family and work. Lim had another reason for carrying on a conversation. He was worried that he himself had a concussion, too.

Right after the collapse, Lim felt elated because he had survived a major catastrophe. But then he thought, *How are we going to get out of here?* He, like the others, wasn't sure how much of the building had collapsed.

In the early minutes of their entombment, Jonas and Battalion Chief Rich Picciotto were sending out Mayday calls on their radios, and not getting any responses. But Lim eventually was able to reach the Port Authority's central command on his radio and tell them that he and 13 others were trapped in the rubble.

When he was asked for their location, Lim used as

a reference point the 25-foot-tall bronze sphere, which had stood in the plaza between the two towers. "Find the globe in the middle of the plaza and then go about 100 yards west, and you'll run right into us," Lim said.

The voice on the other end of the transmission said, "What globe? There is none." It had been smashed and buried under a mountain of debris.

As the hours passed, Lim was wondering if any of the survivors would ever get out. Although cell phone service couldn't connect to phone numbers in the city, he got through to his wife, Diane, at their suburban home in Lynbrook, New York. He told her he was okay. Actually, he was nagged by the thought that rescuers might never find them. But he didn't want to alarm his wife. He just wanted to hear her voice, knowing that if he should die there, at least he had a chance to say good-bye to her first.

Lim then handed the cell phone to the others so they could call their loved ones.

Meanwhile, he worried about the fate of his partner, Sirius. Several times, he radioed central command asking for somebody to check on his dog. But given the enormity of the situation, his request was low on the list of priorities for rescuers.

To help shove aside thoughts of death, Lim, like many of the firefighters, focused on Josephine. They spent most of their time trying to keep her calm and comfortable. Their number one goal was to get her out of this tomb alive.

Five hours after the collapse, Lim and the others discovered a hole above the fifth-floor landing that led to their freedom. Emerging into the daylight, Lim got his first look at the 16 acres of rubble of what had been two magnificent twin towers. He turned to Picciotto and said, "Chief, what do you think the chances of surviving something like this are?"

"One in a billion," Picciotto replied. "One in a billion."

After Lim helped Meldrum over the dangerous, smoldering debris field, they were checked over by paramedics at the scene. Covered from head to toe in gray dust, Lim was in shock from his ordeal and feeling pain in his back and head. But he refused to go to the hospital. He first needed to find out if Sirius was okay.

He walked toward 7 WTC and planned to enter the lower level and take the underground walkway to the basement of what was left of the South Tower. But 7 WTC was fully engulfed by flames and in danger of collapsing (which it did about three hours later). Firefighters stopped him, and one of them said, "You can't go in there."

Lim replied, "I don't care. I need to get my dog." *They're looking at me like I am crazy. Well, I don't care how many firefighters there are. They're not going to stop me.* "I'm going in there."

Seeing the determination on Lim's grime-encrusted face, the firefighter moved aside and said, "Okay, do what you have to do."

As he started down the ramp, he was met by

Port Authority cops Lieutenant Bill Dobrowski, Officer Aaron Greenstein, and Officer Bobby Greff. They were overjoyed that he was alive. "We were ready to report you dead," Dobrowski said.

Despite Lim's pleadings to search for Sirius, they convinced him that it was impossible to reach the dog under all the debris. They put him in their car and drove him to the command post. When he walked inside, everyone stood up and cheered because he was the first Port Authority officer to have survived the collapse. (Over the next 12 hours, fellow cops Will Jimeno and John McLoughlin, who had been outside the North Tower when it fell, would be pulled out of the rubble.)

Reluctantly, Lim agreed to be taken to St. Vincent's Hospital, where he was treated for leg and back injuries and a mild concussion. During his brief stay, he saw his wife and two children in an emotional reunion.

"Where's Sirius?" his son, Michael, asked.

"They'll get to him as soon as they can," Lim replied. "They have to rescue any survivors first."

After a few hours at the hospital, Lim told his family, "I'm not hurt very bad. I should go home and free up the hospital bed for all the victims coming in."

Michael looked out the window and said, "What victims?" Outside, doctors and nurses were milling around, waiting for ambulances that never came. Although Lim knew some of the injured were taken to hospitals closer to the WTC, he expected many to arrive at St. Vincent's.

Then it dawned on him: *You either made it out safely, or you were dead.*

Against his doctor's wishes, Lim checked himself out of the hospital and went home with his family. Later that night, Diane told him, "Maybe I should stay up and keep a watch on you."

"Don't worry," he replied. "I'm not going to sleep." He was too keyed up after all that he had gone through, so he spent most of the night watching news coverage of the catastrophe.

While slowly recovering at home, Lim yearned for word that Sirius had been found alive. He knew it would take a miracle. He also knew miracles happen, having experienced one with 13 others in Stairwell B. But when a week went by without any news on Sirius's fate, Lim was forced to accept the cold, hard truth: His loyal partner and beloved pet was dead.

Although Lim was heartbroken, the dog's death was far overshadowed by the human tragedy of 9/11 . . . and by his own incredible survival. For Lim, the miracle of Stairwell B strengthened the faith that he and his family shared. A case in point:

On the morning of the attack, shortly after Lim first called Diane to tell her he was helping evacuate people out of the North Tower, she watched TV in horror as the building collapsed. Trembling in grief, she called her father, Robert Glaser, in West Virginia and cried, "I think I've lost my husband!" Glaser, a Presbyterian minister, told her, "I'll get in touch with my congregation, and we'll pray for him." An hour later, Lim called Diane from Stairwell B telling her he had survived the collapse and was waiting to be rescued. Diane immediately called her father. Upon hearing the amazing news, her relieved dad told her, "I've seen prayer work before, but never *this* fast."

The Port Authority Police Department suffered the greatest single-day loss of life in law enforcement history on 9/11. Thirty-seven officers from every rank were killed at the WTC. Among them were David Lim's three senior officers whom he insisted go ahead of him down Stairwell B: Chief James Romito, Captain Kathy Mazza, and Lieutenant Robert Cirri. An additional 47 Port Authority civilian employees died in the attack.

"I knew about half of those who were killed," Lim says. "I had survivor's guilt, because some of the people I urged to go in front of me died. Time heals all wounds, but it leaves a lot of scars."

Six weeks after the terrorist attack, Lim returned to work part-time. Three months later, on January 22, 2002, he received a phone call that searchers had located Sirius's remains. The dog was found under his master's spare shirt that had fallen off a hook in his office when the building collapsed. The evidence indicated that Sirius had died instantly.

The remains were already in a body bag when Lim arrived at the scene. He chose not to view the body because he wanted to remember Sirius the way he was when he was alive.

Before the dog was removed from the area, they summoned a priest who said a prayer about all creatures great and small. Then, in the same ritual accorded a deceased firefighter or police officer, an American flag was draped over the body bag. As Sirius's remains were brought out, the workers stopped, lined up, and saluted the dog.

Accompanied by Lim, the body was taken in a Port Authority emergency-services vehicle to Bellevue Hospital for an autopsy. On the way there, the truck drove past the various Port Authority police commands where officers stood outside and saluted in honor of the only K-9 to die at the WTC.

When Lim was given Sirius's flag at Bellevue, he broke down and cried. Moments later, the medical examiner, who up until then had been analyzing human body parts for months without showing any emotion, couldn't restrain herself anymore. She wept openly for the first time after seeing the dog's remains.

"Sirius and I were very close," says Lim, who keeps the dog's ashes in an oak urn at home. "No matter where I went, he went. Whatever I asked him to do, he did. He never complained. Sometimes we'd be working for long hours, searching hundreds of cars or trucks, and he'd just look at me like, 'What do you want me to do next?'"

When there was talk of having a memorial for Sirius, Lim insisted that it would be held only after all the other memorials were done for the WTC casualties. "I didn't want anyone to think that I put my dog above any of the victims of 9/11," says Lim.

On April 24, 2002, about 400 people, plus 100 K-9 teams from all over the country, attended a memorial service at Liberty State Park in New Jersey for the fallen Labrador. A dog run was later named in Sirius's honor at Kowsky Plaza in Battery Park City near Ground Zero. "He did the job like the rest of us, and gave his life that day," says Lim. "In my mind, he'll always be a hero."

Lim eventually returned to work full-time, teaming up with a black Labrador retriever named Sprig until 2005, when Lim was promoted to sergeant and the dog was retired as the family pet. Lim, who was promoted to lieutenant in 2008, still works at the Port Authority facilities in New York and New Jersey. After 30 years on the force, he says, "I will retire on my terms, and not because of what some knucklehead from Afghanistan [referring to al-Qaeda leader Osama bin Laden] did to the World Trade Center."

"Don't Jump! We're Coming!"

LIEUTENANT ROSARIO "ROSS" TERRANOVA
Emergency Medical Service

Lieutenant Ross Terranova looked up at the flaming, smoking upper floors of the North Tower and watched death fall from the sky.

At first he thought he was seeing debris tumbling out of the broken windows. But within seconds he realized that those objects were people—doomed people who chose to die from a ten-second plunge that would kill them instantly on impact. Intense smoke and heat had pushed them to this last desperate act of their lives. They jumped alone or in pairs, some holding hands.

It was almost too much for Terranova to bear. "Don't do it!" he screamed at them until he was hoarse. "Don't jump! We're coming!" He knew they couldn't hear him, not when they were more than 1,000 feet above him, not when his voice was drowned out by the din of emergency vehicles on the ground and a raging fire on the top floors.

I can't imagine what's going through their minds, he thought.

They wouldn't stop jumping.

Terranova told himself that although those trapped in the floors above the fire couldn't be saved, thousands more could. As an officer of FDNY's Emergency Medical Service (EMS), he was determined to help ensure that all the injured who made it out were given swift treatment at the scene.

Terranova had been in the Chief of Department's office that morning when he heard Chief Peter Ganci yell, "A plane just hit the World Trade Center!" At first, Terranova assumed it was a joke, but when he looked out the window, he saw smoke billowing out of the upper floors of the North Tower a mile and a half away.

The first thing he did was go to the bathroom, because he figured he wouldn't get another chance for quite a while. Then he alerted his immediate supervisor, three-star chief Jerry Gombo. After grabbing radios and other supplies, the two hopped into a car and, with Terranova driving, sped toward the WTC in a five-vehicle convoy led by Ganci, the highest-ranking officer in the FDNY.

It would be EMS's responsibility to set up medical treatment areas at the scene. Its 2,500 members, including EMTs and paramedics (who are highly skilled EMTs), were used to responding to an average of 3,000 calls for assistance every day. But nothing would compare to what they were about to face.

On the short ride to the WTC, neither Terranova nor Gombo said much, but they were both thinking the same thing: *It'll be a long and difficult day, the most challenging in the history of the EMS.*

They split off from the others and parked on Fulton and Church Streets east of the complex near St. Paul's Chapel. Bolting from the car, they entered a world of chaos. People were running out of the North Tower. A few paramedics and EMTs were already treating dazed victims just east of the building in a makeshift triage area. Emergency vehicles were roaring to the scene from all directions.

It's going to be bad, but we can handle it, Terranova thought. *Everyone will get out safely, the injured will get treated, and the firefighters will knock down the fire.*

Trained as an EMT, Terranova treated a few victims, including a man whose head was bleeding. But as a lieutenant, Terranova's role was to help organize the department's dozens of arriving EMTs and paramedics so they could do their jobs effectively. With a trace of reluctance, he turned his patients over to an EMT.

Surveying the scene, Terranova urged the fleeing office workers to keep moving away from the building. People were asking, "What's happening? What's going on?" He didn't have time to explain. As respectfully as he could, he told them, "Just keep moving north. Get as far away as you can." Some people were so dazed they stood still, staring straight up. "Keep moving!" he ordered. "Don't look!"

In the strange snow of fluttering paper, debris of various sizes kept crashing to the ground. It was obvious to Terranova that the triage area was in a dangerous location. "We're too close to the building," he told the EMTs. "Let's evacuate." As increasing amounts of rubble bombed the spot, he and Gombo helped move patients farther away.

Tragically, some people didn't or couldn't move fast enough and were seriously injured or fatally crushed by the falling fragments. A massive piece of burning metal slammed within a few yards of Terranova.

They established a safer triage area across Church Street near the chapel. From his vantage point on the east side, Terranova tried to convince himself that the damage to the North Tower didn't look so terrible. But he discovered it was actually worse after he and Gombo hurried to the west side of the North Tower to coordinate efforts with Ganci.

That's when Terranova first saw people leaping to their deaths. Instinctively, he yelled and pleaded for them to stop. But his shouts were in vain. Never had he felt more helpless and more hopeless. *If I only had a megaphone. Who am I kidding; they can't hear me. I wish I could do something. But I can't. None of us can. It's a lost cause.*

They wouldn't stop jumping.

Terranova forced himself to focus on those who could be saved. *I have a job to do,* he told himself, *so let's go forward with the mission and do the best we can.*

He and Gombo went inside the North Tower lobby to the command post, where a plan was put together to establish staging areas to treat and evacuate patients. Terranova figured there would be hundreds, if not thousands, of people needing medical assistance.

Because of serious communications problems and radio interference, Ganci moved the command post outside and across West Street near 2 World Financial Center. As the EMS officers were setting up, they heard a low-flying second jetliner zooming in from the south. Seconds later, it tore into the South Tower, causing a violent blast and fireball.

At the moment of impact, the stunned EMS group at the new command center felt an intense flash of heat generated from the explosion, even though it was hundreds of yards away. Fiery debris began cascading onto West Street.

"My God, we're under attack!" Terranova shouted to no one in particular. *What are we going to do now?* he wondered. Then he answered his own question: *Just do our jobs.*

Meanwhile, the pace of the civilians exiting both towers increased rapidly, but for the most part remained orderly despite a growing sense of disbelief.

Less than an hour after the second plane struck,

First Deputy Fire Commissioner Bill Feehan approached Terranova at the outdoor EMS command center and asked, "Any idea how many patients we'll be treating?"

"I don't know," Terranova replied. "Many of them are still trapped . . ."

He stopped in mid-sentence after hearing Ganci shout, "Oh no!"

Spinning on his heels, Terranova looked toward the South Tower. To his utter shock, the building was starting to collapse.

Ganci hollered, "Go! Go! Go!"

I don't think I can outrun this, Terranova thought. *I've got to find cover.*

He had a choice: run to the right, as some were already doing, or run to the left. He chose left. Turning to Gombo, he said, "Jerry, let's get to cover!" Terranova took about four giant strides and looked over his shoulder. Gombo hadn't moved. He seemed transfixed at the unbelievable sight of a 110-story building crumbling to the ground.

Terranova ran back, grabbed Gombo by the collar of his shirt, and yanked him to the left. They dashed to a nearby ramp that led down to a loading dock of the nearest building and crouched behind a parked white van.

Terranova couldn't help himself. There was still a part of him that just had to see what was happening, so he stood up for a quick glimpse. *Wow, the building is going down right before my eyes. It doesn't seem possible.* Amid a thunderous rumble that grew into a roar unlike any he had ever heard before, he saw an ominous billowing cloud churning toward him.

He hunkered behind the truck as thousands of pounds of rubble rained onto the ramp in a deafening racket that jangled every fiber of his body. Then came silence and darkness.

It was what he imagined death would be like—a sinister stillness wrapped in a creepy gloom. But he knew he wasn't dead. *Thank God I'm alive.* Realizing he had been holding his breath since the ramp filled with smothering dust, he inhaled. Pain ripped at his lungs and throat as if he was breathing sand. He gasped for air. *I can't believe I got away from the collapse, and now I'm going to suffocate to death. What a horrible way to go.* He pulled his T-shirt over his nose and mouth, hoping it would help him breathe. It did, but barely. Every time he took a breath, his mouth filled with soot, powder, and pulverized cement. And it hurt.

Although he couldn't see Gombo, he could feel him moving. *Okay, there are at least two of us who are still alive.*

Gombo always carried a small flashlight in his pocket, because he figured there would be unexpected times when he would need one. This was one of those times. He turned it on. To Terranova, who was right next to him, the beam was only slightly visible in the swirling dust.

"Ross, are you all right?" Gombo asked between coughs.

"Yeah. I'm not hurt. Just hard to breathe. And you?"

"I'm okay. We should get up and try to find a way out of here."

Terranova began feeling jittery because the vehicle they had been hiding behind was a white van with no markings. It was the same kind of truck that terrorists had packed with explosives and blown up in the North Tower's underground parking garage in 1993. "We're not in a good spot here, Jerry."

As the dust settled, they could see that the entrance to the ramp was blocked by debris. They called out to anyone who might have been trapped in the rubble, but didn't hear any reply. So they headed toward the back of the loading dock, where they met up with several other first-responders who had sought safety.

They crowded into the booth of the dock supervisor and shoved a towel under the door to keep out the dust. Taking turns using a water cooler, they rinsed gunk out of their mouths, which allowed them to breathe and talk easier. They didn't have any radio communication. Their cell phones and the office phone didn't work, either.

The group found a way out of the building by going through an exit on the west side, which opened onto a marina and World Financial Center Plaza. To Terranova, it seemed like such a different world than it was on the other side of the building. Here, sailboats moored to the docks rocked gently in the water. Large umbrellas shaded the tables and chairs of outdoor cafés. Everything seemed so quiet and peaceful, as though it was a thousand miles away from the bedlam only a block away. But everything was also coated in a dusty gray.

Terranova and Gombo walked a block north to the Embassy Suites Hotel at the corner of Vesey Street and North End Avenue. In the lobby, an EMS treatment area had been set up to care for a few injured firefighters and several civilians.

The pair headed outside again, walking on Vesey Street toward the command center, wondering if it would still be there. A snow of gray ash and pieces of paper continued to fall, covering the ground and creating a bizarre winterlike landscape.

They encountered some paramedics on the street treating injured civilians. "This isn't safe here," Terranova told them. "You need to move farther away. You don't know what else can happen."

"We'll finish up with these patients first, and then we'll evacuate," replied one of the paramedics.

Suddenly, Terranova heard an awful thundering roar. It was the same sound that had accompanied the collapse of the South Tower. He looked up. *Oh my God, now the North Tower is collapsing!* As the racket intensified, Terranova began pushing people on the street, shouting, "Move! Move! Move! The North Tower is falling!"

Keeping his eyes on the tumbling skyscraper, Terranova backpedaled furiously while warning everyone to seek shelter. Then he saw a treacherous gray cloud rolling like a killer tidal wave down the street directly toward him. He yelled at everyone he saw, "Follow me!" Then he sprinted toward the Embassy Suites.

He saw that some panicky people were running down the sidewalk rather than ducking into doorways. So he stationed himself at the corner of the building. That way he could step out, grab them, and pull them off to the side before the cloud engulfed them.

Braced for the galloping cloud, Terranova pressed himself face-first against the building. But no matter how hard he clung, he was no match for the powerful force that was propelling the cloud. As it churned past him, he was pulled away from the building and knocked off his feet. Fortunately, he wasn't hit with any debris.

Once again, he had to cover his mouth and nose with his T-shirt to help him breathe. After the dust thinned out, he looked at the spot where he had last seen paramedics treating the injured on the street. Now there was nothing but rubble. *I hope they got out in time,* he thought.

He and Gombo returned to the hotel lobby and, after a while, noticed that most of the EMTs were no longer busy. *Where are all the victims?* Terranova wondered. *There should be hundreds of them. Now it seems like there's nobody left to treat.* He had a sinking feeling that the collapse of the two towers had killed most everyone who hadn't escaped. He feared that what was currently a rescue effort for the injured would soon become a recovery effort for the dead.

At least our people and everyone who made it here are in a safe location. Nothing else is likely to fall. He and

Gombo were developing a new plan when he noticed police and firefighters running away from the hotel. He rushed outside, grabbed a police officer by the arm, and asked, "What's going on?"

"There's a major gas leak in the building."

Terranova darted inside and warned everyone to evacuate. He told Gombo, "We need to move again. It's no longer safe here."

Gombo agreed, saying, "We can't put our people in harm's way. Let's get everyone to move north, and then we'll regroup and figure out our next plan."

Because communications were still ineffective, Gombo decided to establish an EMS command post at police headquarters about eight blocks east so he could coordinate with other agencies and city services. On the way there, Gombo, said, "The first two calls we'll make are to Rena [Gombo's wife] and Kristin [Terranova's fiancée]. Then we're going to get to work."

After they arrived, Terranova called Kristin, a music teacher at an elementary school on Long Island, and told her, "I'm okay. I'm not hurt, but I'll be here until late tonight."

"Be safe and take all the time you need," she told him.

He and Gombo spent the balance of the first day setting up a work schedule and long-term operation. While at the headquarters, Terranova had his first chance to see on TV the stunning images of the destruction of the WTC and the Pentagon, and the impact zone where the fourth hijacked plane crashed in Pennsylvania. Only then did he fully understand the magnitude of the terrorist attacks.

Like all members of the FDNY, Terranova and Gombo were in a state of shock as news trickled in of the mounting number of presumed deaths of New York's Bravest—one hundred . . . two hundred . . . three hundred . . . and counting.

How lucky am I, Terranova pondered. *I'm wearing a short-sleeve uniform shirt and a helmet. No jacket. No safety boots. No protective clothing. I survived the collapse of two buildings, and I don't have a scratch on me.*

At about 10 P.M., he and Gombo left for the night to look for their car. On the way, they met Captain Jimmy "Yak" Yakimovich, a big burly veteran firefighter. He was slumped over, looking like a broken man. His eyes watering, he told Terranova, "They're all dead. Ganci, Feehan, Burns." The devastated captain was referring to three of the top leaders in the FDNY—Chief of Department Peter Ganci, First Deputy Fire Commissioner Bill Feehan, and Assistant Chief Donald Burns.

"Yes, Yak, it's a tragedy," Terranova said. He had learned earlier about those deaths, but hearing someone saying it with such sorrow packed a powerful emotional punch.

Trudging onward, he and Gombo found their dust-covered car. It was scratched up but otherwise intact, except for one broken window. In fact, they noticed that the windows of several parked cars had been smashed. "I think I know why," Terranova told Gombo. "People who were caught in one of the debris clouds after the collapse probably broke the windows and took gulps of clean air that were in the cars."

Terranova went home for a few hours of sleep and then returned to Ground Zero by 6 A.M., where searchers were painstakingly probing the pile of rubble and exploring voids for any survivors. Later that morning, when none of the hundreds of missing firefighters had been pulled out alive, his hopes began to fade that any would be rescued.

The grief only got worse for Terranova while sitting in a temporary command post studying page after page of a list of first-responders who weren't accounted for. His eyes fell on the name of Mike Mullan. *Oh, God, not him.* Mullan, a firefighter from Ladder 12, was a good friend since their high school days. After Mullan had learned in 1985 that Terranova's sister Marie, who is physically disabled, had a crush on him, he always sent her flowers on her birthday. He never missed a year, even when he was deployed as a captain in the Army Reserves. (Marie still keeps a photo of Mullan in her room.)

It seemed every week over the next 18 months, there was another funeral, another memorial that Terranova attended. He would don his dress uniform and go to nearby towns and cities to honor those brave men and women of 9/11, many of whom he didn't know personally. If he never heard another rendition of "Amazing Grace," it would be too soon.

He, like hundreds of members of the FDNY who were at the scene before the collapse of the two towers, was awarded the World Trade Center Survivor Medal. The gold medal dangles from a purple and black ribbon. Above it is a rectangular citation bar. The left half of the bar shows the number 343 in gold (for the number of FDNY members killed) against a purple background. The right half displays two gold stars on a black background.

In 2002, at the funeral of a fallen firefighter, Terranova was talking with Daniel Nigro, who had assumed the position Chief of Department after the death of his close friend Peter Ganci. Because the chief was a highly decorated veteran, he was authorized to wear an impressive number of citations and medals on his dress uniform. But Terranova noticed that Nigro was wearing only one—the World Trade Center Survivor Medal.

"Chief," Terranova asked, "why aren't you wearing all your medals?"

Nigro pointed to the lone medal and replied, "After 9/11, this is the only one that matters."

Ross Terranova was promoted to captain in 2003. Three years later, he was named a deputy chief of the NYFD's EMS Command.

In the months after 9/11, Terranova tried to ease the heartache of that day by working long hours. "I had to work because that was my therapy," he explains. "I was working with people who knew what I was going through, because they had gone through it, too. More importantly, I figured that if I was working for the good of others, maybe it would somewhat make up for those I couldn't help on 9/11."

He often sees Jerry Gombo, now deputy assistant chief of EMS Operations. "We have a standing date on September 11," Terranova says. "We go together to the annual memorial service and then spend time at Ground Zero and retrace our route. Every time I see him on September 11, he pulls out his flashlight, waves it, and then puts it away." No words are spoken. None are needed.

What happened on 9/11 has taught Terranova, the married father of three, how fickle life can be. "Sometimes you have to make a life-or-death decision in a split second—like do you run to the left or to the right," he says. "I've always been haunted by the fact that everyone at our command center who went left when the South Tower fell survived. Those who ran right ultimately died." Although First Deputy Fire Commissioner Bill Feehan and Chief of Department Peter Ganci escaped from the first collapse, they later perished when the North Tower fell. "Had we followed them and gone to the right during the South Tower's collapse, we likely would have stayed with them and would have died when the North Tower came down," Terranova says.

He adds that it was his duty to attend as many funerals as he could. "If it had been me who had died, others would have stood the line for me." He's referring to the custom of members of the department who stand at attention on one side of the street and face the place of worship during the funeral procession for a fallen comrade. "Going to their funerals or memorials was my way to honor them. These people made the ultimate sacrifice that I hope I will never have to make. And they deserve to be honored for that. It was just their fate that they chose to make a right instead of a left."

"Where Do I Begin to Look?"

FIREFIGHTER KEVIN MURRAY, JR.
Fire Department of New York

Caked from head to toe in gray ash, firefighter Kevin Murray stared at the ruins of the Twin Towers.

It is all so unreal.

The two 1,300-foot-tall structures had been reduced to a pile of twisted steel, busted concrete, and gnarled building materials crammed in a heap five stories above and six stories below the ground.

Where do I begin to look?

Somewhere in Ground Zero, he hoped to find some sign, some clue, that his missing firehouse brothers from Ladder 11 would be found alive. Maybe, he hoped, they were huddling in a void awaiting rescue. Or maybe they were spared by fate just like the 14 survivors who emerged from Stairwell B earlier in the day. Or maybe, just maybe, they escaped from one of the towers as it collapsed in the same way Murray had done. After all, their company was nicknamed the Lucky 11.

I have to search for them. I have to try.

So he climbed carefully onto the pile. He picked his way across dust-covered, 40-foot-long steel beams that lay scattered like toothpicks. He peered into cavities that were still belching smoke. He moved aside chunks of cement and wedges of sheet metal. No matter where he looked, the results were the same. He found nothing, at least nothing identifiable.

Where are the desks and the chairs and the comput-ers? Everything has been pulverized. If I can't find any furniture or office equipment that I can recognize in this debris, how am I ever going to find anyone alive?

The day couldn't have started out better. A beautiful, clear morning greeted early-risers like Murray. On his way to the fire station that houses Ladder 11, he dropped off his father, Kevin Murray, Sr., in front of the North Tower, where the elder Murray worked for Instinet, a financial communications firm.

Less than an hour later, the life of the 27-year-old firefighter would change forever.

Moments after the North Tower was struck by a hijacked jetliner, Murray rushed over to nearby Ladder 18 to fill out its roster, which was short one man. He joined Lieutenant Gary Borega, Charlie Maloney, Harry Coyle, Steve Merenda, Ralph Cardino, and Hugh Mettham.

"Where Do I Begin to Look?"

As their hook-and-ladder raced to the scene, the second plane struck the South Tower. They all sensed they were rushing into a calamity much larger than anything they had ever experienced. Murray didn't know what to expect. *Will there be more jets? Will there be more targets?* But those thoughts took a backseat to his biggest concern: His father. *Is Dad hurt? Is he dead? Did he get out? If not, will he?*

After their rig parked on the west side of the North Tower, the men from Ladder 18 scurried toward the building's entrance, dodging falling debris along the way. But Murray was so worried about his father that he wasn't paying attention to what was dropping from above. *I've got to find Dad and make sure. . . .*

"Kevin, look out!" shouted one of his comrades.

Instinctively, Murray jumped back just in time to avoid being killed by a person who was falling to his death.

Near the entrance, Murray and two others helped Father Mychal Judge, the department's popular chaplain, through a large broken window. "God bless you," said the priest. "Be careful."

Once inside the lobby, the men received their orders from fire commissioner Tom Von Essen: "Don't worry about the fire. Just go up and help get people out of here." The commissioner didn't say what the men already suspected. Those poor souls who were trapped above the fire couldn't be saved.

"Everyone, stay together," said Borega. Murray

had brought along a rabbit tool (a portable hydraulic device designed to pull apart twisted wreckage) and also a search rope. If they encountered a smoky area, he would tie the rope to an exit door and hold on to the rope while doing a search so he wouldn't get lost. The men had brought extra cylinders of oxygen for their self-contained breathing apparatuses (SCBAs) into the lobby. When they learned they would be using the stairs, they decided to leave the tanks behind because of the extra weight. They knew they would have to conserve their energy during the climb.

As the damaged lobby filled with firefighters, Murray glanced over at Father Judge, who was walking over to the various companies and praying for their safety.

Before heading up the stairs, the men from Ladder 18 checked several of the building's 99 elevators to make sure no one was trapped. When the plane had struck, some of the elevators automatically went to the lobby level, but the damaged doors locked up. The firefighters pried open the doors, freeing several people who had no clue that the towers had been attacked.

The men then marched up the stairs. Every so often, Murray would ask people who were going down, "Anyone from Instinet? Does anyone know what floor Instinet is on?" The only responses he received were blank stares or shaking heads.

Radio communications were bad, but one message got through: "There's a third plane coming our way. Evacuate!" The men of Ladder 18 ignored it. Civilians were still tromping down the stairs, so there was no way the firefighters would flee and leave them behind. (The report was erroneous.)

Jet fuel that had sprayed into the elevator shafts had ignited small fires on many of the floors, triggering the sprinkler heads. Water dribbled down the stairs and caused sheetrock on various floors to crumble.

Murray had reached the tenth floor in Stairwell B when unexpectedly the building began to shake violently, causing some of his comrades to stumble because the floor was rocking. Smoke and dust whirled up the stairway, and all the lights went out. At first Murray wondered if the entire building was going to topple. But then the frightening movement stopped.

People in the stairs were screaming, crying, and whimpering. Some panicked and shouted, "We're all going to die!"

The men from Ladder 18 didn't know what had happened. Rumors spread in the stairwell: Another plane had struck the North Tower. . . . The sixty-fifth floor had collapsed. . . . A bomb in the building had exploded. With radio communications spotty at best, they didn't know that the South Tower had collapsed.

Murray tried to calm people's fears. "Don't worry," he told them. "It's probably just a localized collapse far above us where the fire is. You'll be fine. Just keep moving." The line now went down at a much faster clip. *Dad, I hope you made it out.*

Because the lights were out and the air was heavily

charged with dust, it was hard to see, so the firefighters spread out at various landings and used their flashlights to guide the office workers down Stairwell B.

Soon the only people going down the stairs were firefighters, including those from Engine 28, who had made it up to the fortieth floor before turning around. When Murray reached the lobby, he was stunned by all the damage he saw—much worse than when he had arrived 90 minutes earlier. The once bright lobby of tan marble and shiny chrome was now littered with rubble, glass, wires, and pipes. Smoke from several small fires curled toward the broken ceiling. Every window had been shattered, and the floor was covered with several inches of pulverized concrete.

My God, what's happened here? It looks like a missile hit the lobby. There was no way for him to know at the time that when the South Tower collapsed, it created a blast of air that burst through the North Tower's lobby and passageways, destroying most everything in its path.

Before Murray had a chance to grasp what he was seeing, a member of Rescue 1, his face and arms trickling with blood, rushed over to the men of Ladder 18 and shouted, "My guys are stuck upstairs! Please, you've got to come up with me if you've got any steam left in you."

The men flashed glances at one another. They knew that they were in the middle of a terrorist attack, that this was no regular fire, that other attacks were possible. But they weren't about to abandon their brethren. So they headed back up. "Boy, we're tempting fate now," said firefighter Ralph Cardino.

At about the eighth floor, they ran into a company of descending firefighters who urged them, "Get out now!" The men from Ladder 18 chose to ignore the warning and continued up, bypassing a few serious fires shooting out from the elevator shafts. The fumes from the jet fuel were getting stronger. Not finding any of the missing firefighters or any more civilians, Lieutenant Borega finally ordered everyone back down.

After they returned to the lobby, the men joined those from six other companies and debated their next move. Some felt they would be safer to remain inside because all the exits were being bombarded by debris and jumpers. Others wanted to rush to their trucks.

Firefighter Roy Chelsen, from Engine 28, bolted for his rig and made it safely. Then he turned around and zigzagged back to the lobby. "The South Tower is gone!" he shouted. "It fell! And it looks like the top fifty floors of this building are fully involved [on fire]. You need to get out of here right now, because it's going to come down any second!"

Forming a line in single file, the men hugged the front of 6 WTC, the building closest to the North Tower, to avoid getting struck from above. They had planned to run to their rig, which was parked under the pedestrian bridge that crossed West Street a few hundred yards northwest of the North Tower.

Within 30 seconds of leaving the lobby, Murray saw

the upper floors of the North Tower were leaning as if the building was melting from the top down. Hearing harsh banging and seeing floors collapsing on each other, he gasped, "My God, it's coming down!" With fellow firefighter Hugh Mettham at his heels, Murray ran north on West Street. *We're in the collapse zone. There's no way we can outrun it. We've got to find cover.*

As he sprinted, he tossed aside his rabbit tool, accidentally smashing the window of a parked van. Even though he was running for his life, he thought, *I'm going to get into trouble for that.* He turned around for a glimpse at the final seconds of the once great structure. Realizing he was out of time, he veered off toward the nearest parked fire truck.

Murray dove under the vehicle for cover, curled up in a ball, and hoped the truck was strong enough to withstand the massive amount of pounding debris. He lay in a fetal position while protecting his eyes and face from pellets of concrete that were bouncing off the street and striking his fire helmet and body.

The cloud of dust and ash cloaked the vehicle. Murray could hardly breathe through the choking dust. *That's it. I'm going to die.* Anger rather than fear washed over him. *I survived the collapse, and now I'm going to suffocate.* Between bouts of holding his breath and wheezing, he felt himself on the edge of losing consciousness.

It turned so dark and silent that at first he thought everyone else was dead. He didn't hear any screams or voices for a minute or two. Then he felt a hand squeeze his leg. It was Mettham, who had slipped under the truck, too.

"Are . . . we . . . trapped . . . or . . . buried?" Murray asked between hacks.

Mettham crawled backward until he was out from under the fire truck. Getting to his feet, he announced, "Kevin, we're not buried."

Murray scrambled out. The darkness had turned to an orange haze through which he could barely make out shadowy figures staggering to their feet.

Mettham said, "We gotta go north."

Murray thought, *Which way is north? Nothing looks like it used to.*

It was still difficult to breathe, so Murray put on his Scott Pack (self-contained breathing apparatus). But it was full of dust. When he inhaled, the dust blew into his eyes and lungs, making it almost impossible to see or breathe. He felt like he was drowning. Trying not to panic, he told himself, *I just have to wait it out.* He nearly lost consciousness before he began sucking in air that became increasingly cleaner with each breath.

Squinting through the haze, Murray and Mettham walked north on West Street in search of the rest of the men of Ladder 18. Along the way, an EMT stopped them and ordered them to sit down on the curb. He poured water on their heads so they could wash out their eyes and mouths.

Then the pair continued to look for their comrades. They found Ralph Cardino's helmet, but no sign of him. *This doesn't look good*, Murray thought.

He tried not to think about the mounting number of deaths of first-responders and innocent civilians. What weighed on him the most was the fate of his father. *There's no way he could have survived the collapse. I sure hope he got out in time. But what if he didn't?*

His thought was broken by the sound of shrieking jet engines. *Oh my God, we're going to get hit again!* People began scrambling in all directions looking for cover as several jets streaked low across the sky. Murray's shot nerves relaxed when he saw that the planes were F-16s from the United States Air Force. Seeing them made him feel confident that there would be no more air attacks in New York City.

He and Mettham entered a school on Murray and West Streets in search of a phone and water. They found both. Murray tried to reach his wife, Stephanie, whom he had married six months earlier. She was working at St. Vincent's Hospital, but its phone lines weren't working at the time. He finally got in touch with his mother and told her he was safe. Then, with his heart pounding with anxiety, he asked, "What about Dad? Did he make it out?"

"Yes, he's fine."

Hearing those words, Murray wept with relief. When he regained his composure, he asked her to keep trying to reach Stephanie and tell her he was okay. (His mother tried but never got through. Stephanie didn't find out that Murray was alive until 7 P.M. when he finally reached her.)

A few minutes later, he and Mettham found the rest of Ladder 18 except for Cardino. After they embraced, Murray was told that the missing Cardino likely had been killed. "We're pretty sure Ralph is gone," said an officer who was reading off a list of names of firefighters who were feared dead.

Seeing the men from Ladder 18 gave Murray hope that maybe his buddies at Ladder 11 had survived. He had to find out, so he went up to company after company, asking everyone if they had seen his firehouse brothers. No one had.

Maybe they're trapped under the rubble. Maybe they're waiting to be rescued. I have to find them.

He headed for the massive debris field and was struck by the enormity of the devastation. Climbing over huge shards of metal and large pieces of concrete, he joined an army of searchers who had no plan, no direction, no orders other than to find anyone in the ruins who might have been blessed with a miracle.

Every few minutes, someone would whistle and raise his hand, signaling for quiet because he thought he heard tapping or a voice under the rubble. Searchers would stop digging and shut off their steel-cutting saws. Search dogs would poke around the spot without distraction. Those moments, although common, were always false alarms.

Every hour, Murray would visit a temporary

command post where firefighters were supposed to check in. The post kept a list of those who were alive as well as those who were missing or confirmed dead. Each time he visited the post, he asked, "Did you find 11 Truck? Any news about 11 Truck?" The answer was always the same: No.

Taking a break, he came across firefighter Bobby Newman from Battalion 1, who told him that he narrowly escaped both collapses. Murray was shocked to see that Newman was barefoot. "What happened to your shoes?" he asked.

"They were blown off my feet when the South Tower collapsed," replied Newman, the aide to Battalion Chief Matthew Ryan. Newman said that shortly before 10 A.M. he had been standing near the entrance of the South Tower while Ryan was conversing with other battalion chiefs at the command post in the lobby of the South Tower. When the building started to fall, the rush of air from the collapse blew Newman across the street—and right out of his shoes. Dazed and hurt, he wandered barefoot looking for help for those buried under the rubble. His radio wasn't working. Less than a half hour later, he was walking past the North Tower when it, too, began to crumble. Once again, he barely escaped with his life. Ryan, however, was killed.

Murray returned to the pile and continued his search. The next few hours were like a blur to him, because the shock from all that he had endured throughout the day had left him physically and mentally spent. What he saw—and more importantly what he didn't see—only added to his misery. He found no signs of life. Hope had turned to despair . . . and then to sorrow.

He learned that Father Mychal Judge, the beloved FDNY chaplain, had been killed by flying debris. Three firefighters who hid under Ladder 18's truck as the North Tower fell were found dead.

Later that night, Murray returned to his firehouse where he received the heartbreaking confirmation that all six of the men from Ladder 11 had perished. They had been on the top floor of the Marriott Hotel, which had stood between the two towers. When the South Tower fell, it took out a huge section of the upper floors of the hotel, crushing the firefighters. Murray was now the only one from Ladder 11 who had survived—and only because he had been detailed to Ladder 18.

Murray wept over the tragic news. Gone were Lieutenant Michael Quilty, 42, who had been on the job for two decades; John Heffernan, 37, who in his free time played guitar in a punk-rock band; Eddie Day, 45, who would slap a smiley-face sticker on the helmet of any sad comrade; Matt Rogan, 37, who was the firehouse's handyman; Richard (Ricky) Kelly, 50, who was the longest-serving man at Ladder 11; and Mike Cammarata, the 22-year-old rookie who had achieved an impressive 105 perfect score on the New York Fireman's Test.

Cammarata was the city's youngest firefighter to die that day. Sworn in on May 3, he had been given shield No. 1138, which his uncle Doug Bartucci had worn proudly for 33 years. On the morning of the attacks, Cammarata, who was nearing the end of his 14-week training program and awaiting official graduation, had asked Murray, "Do you want me to take your detail on 18 Truck?" Murray had replied, "No, that's okay. I'll do it."

What if I had said yes? Murray thought.

One of the few positive moments for Murray that evening was learning that Ralph Cardino wasn't killed after all. Cardino was in the hospital undergoing treatment for a serious leg injury suffered during the collapse of the North Tower.

The next morning, Murray returned to Ground Zero and continued to search for possible survivors, even though he believed that if he found anyone it would likely be only a body. His anguish was so deep that at times it clouded his judgment, causing him to take unnecessary risks. He would tie his rope to a beam and lower himself 30 or more feet into a dark and dangerous void. He ignored the real possibility that the rubble overhead could shift and trap or fatally crush him. Once inside the cavelike space, he would weave his way around chemical fires and call out, "Anybody here?" No one ever responded. Sometimes he couldn't go up the way he came down and had to find another way out, often squeezing through tight cavities and fissures.

Over the next three weeks, he scoured over and under the debris field every other day on a demanding 24-hour shift—four hours on, one hour off. His yellow and black turnout gear had turned gray from the heavy concentrations of dust that rose whenever the rubble was disturbed. He had no respirator, only a cheap paper face mask to minimize the junk he was breathing in. He soon developed a persistent hacking cough.

Day after day, his senses were assaulted until they became numb. His nose rebelled against the stench of death that saturated Ground Zero. His bloodshot eyes stung from the constant dust. His mouth, lips, and tongue were coated with grime. His ears rang from the raucous pounding of jackhammers, loud droning of generators, and high-pitched screeching of circular saws cutting through steel beams. His hands and arms were scratched from the sharp edges of sheet metal and rebar.

Despite the agony and the grief he felt daily, Murray continued to work the pile just like thousands of others — firefighters, police officers, National Guardsmen, Army Reservists, ironworkers, volunteers, and civilian contractors.

Everywhere he looked, he saw the one symbol that embodied the reason why they put their heart and soul into their efforts. It waved on poles above the rubble and over crushed fire trucks. It flapped from nearby buildings and lampposts. It fluttered off of cranes and scaffolding. It stood out on helmets and uniforms.

Everywhere he looked, Kevin Murray saw the American flag.

Firefighter Kevin Murray, the married father of three, remains a member of Ladder 11.

He was one of more than 90,000 rescue, recovery, and clean-up workers who were exposed to the environmental hazards at Ground Zero during their work on the pile. Thousands reported developing asthma after working at the WTC site. FDNY first-responders showed serious health issues soon after the attacks because they were exposed to chemical fires and dust composed mainly of ground-up concrete, glass, fiberglass, and asbestos.

Murray was put on light duty for two years after losing 40 percent of his lung capacity (the volume of air exhaled from a deep breath). "From 2003 to 2005, I was basically told I wouldn't be a firefighter again," he recalls. "But I refused to quit. I finally got the outside medical care I needed. I still don't have the lung capacity I used to have, but it's now back to eighty-five percent.

"What happened on 9/11 and the weeks afterward were like part of a never-ending nightmare, almost like it didn't really happen. It left me emotionally, mentally, and physically drained. I went through a lot of counselors, sometimes visiting them three or four times a week." He says he had to work through many issues before he could return to active duty as a firefighter. "It's therapeutic for me to be doing the job I love," he adds. "I need to be a firefighter. It's a way to give back to the guys who lost their lives."

"Oh No! Not Again!"

DETECTIVE SERGEANT MIKE KOSOWSKI
New York Police Department

NYPD Detective Sergeant Mike Kosowski was at his desk in the First Precinct, talking on the phone to his brother, John, when he heard the throbbing whine of jet engines. The noise grew louder. While he continued his conversation, his brain was warning him that something wasn't right, so he looked out his window.

Kosowski was startled to see a commercial airliner flying dangerously low, banking in from the north. The pitch of the engines quickly changed to a shrieking roar as the jet blasted over the precinct.

"John, a jet plane just flew by, and it's so low that it's not going to clear the buildings!" blurted Kosowski. "I've got to go!" He hung up. Less than a minute later, the precinct's phones started ringing with reports that a plane had crashed into the North Tower of the WTC.

Kosowski, 46, who was the supervisor of detectives for the First Division, summoned Officer Joe Cosaluzzo and police detective Hugh McGough. Dressed in sports coats and ties with detective shields dangling from their necks, the trio jumped in a car and sped down West Broadway toward the WTC, which was only a half mile away.

They were stopped by patrol sergeant Robert Sprague a couple of blocks north of the complex. Kosowski noticed that Sprague, who was in his midtwenties, looked as though he had aged ten years from shock. "Can you hold down the street for emergency evacuation?" Sprague asked.

"Sure, we'll help out any way we can," Kosowski replied. He assumed the crash was a terrible accident and figured he and his partners would end up having to notify families of the victims. "It's going to be an awful day."

Office workers poured out of the burning North Tower by the thousands. While urging them to keep moving away from the WTC, Kosowski and his partners diverted traffic to make evacuation easier and create better access for emergency vehicles.

Suddenly, they heard an explosion. Kosowski wheeled around, but couldn't tell what had happened. An older man rushed up to him and shouted, "My God! A second plane just struck the World Trade Center, this time into the South Tower!"

"Oh No! Not Again!"

Kosowski felt a pit in his stomach. He knew immediately that it was a terrorist attack. For the previous ten days, the NYPD had been put on heightened security because intelligence reports had warned that terrorists were plotting to strike the United States. But no one knew how or when.

Leaving McGough and Cosaluzzo to handle the traffic, Kosowski and Captain Peter Winski, First Precinct commanding officer, hurried down to the corner of West and Vesey Streets. There, a gathering crowd was staring at the debris and at victims falling from the towers. Many of the bystanders cried in anguish as they watched hopeless people from the blazing upper floors plunge to their deaths.

With Kosowski taking the left side of the street and Winski the right side, the two worked their way south along West Street, trying to clear the area in front of both towers. Some in the crowd were so riveted by what they were witnessing that Kosowski had to shake them to force them to move away.

After he and Winski split up, Kosowski headed for the North Tower to see how he could help. But it wasn't easy. He was getting pelted with broken glass and had to dodge the falling debris and the jumpers. When he entered the building, a firefighter stopped him and said, "Sarge, we're evacuating. Don't bother coming in here. The building is rocking. We've got to get out of here."

Kosowski retreated to West and Vesey Streets and tried to use his cell phone to call the precinct, but couldn't get through. A firefighter next to him pointed to the World Financial Center (WFC) across the street and said, "If you need a phone, use the hard line over there." Then, half in earnest, he said, "If you get a hold of someone, tell him to send the army."

On his way to the WFC, Kosowski spotted a man of Indian descent on his knees praying in the middle of West Street in front of the South Tower. "You need to get out of here," said the detective sergeant.

"Leave me alone," the man replied tearfully. Pointing to the building, he explained, "My wife is up there on the eighty-second floor."

Kosowski grabbed the man's arm and lifted him to his feet. "Look, sir, you must move away right now. You're in danger here."

"No, I can't."

"Do you have kids?"

"Yes."

"Okay. You don't know if your wife is still up there or if she got out. Let's say she's trapped and dies and because you won't move, you're killed from falling debris. How would either of you feel if nobody was home to take care of your children?"

The man nodded and reluctantly let Kosowski escort him to an EMT, who took him out of the danger zone.

Kosowski went into the WFC to an area in the back corner of the ground level, where he came upon two security guards, ten civilians, and NYPD Lieutenant Roger Parrino.

"Oh No! Not Again!"

Using the landline, Kosowski called the Manhattan borough command's detective office and asked for more personnel to meet at West and Vesey Streets. "There are already deaths and many injuries," he said. A lieutenant ordered him to spearhead a temporary headquarters about a mile away in the Fifth Precinct. Before hanging up, the lieutenant told Kosowski, "Mike, you've got to get everybody out of there, because eight to eleven more planes are still in the air. If any of them have been hijacked . . ." The lieutenant didn't have to finish his sentence. Kosowski knew that if there were more terrorists in the sky, more attacks were likely at this site.

He gave a quick call to his wife, Fran, who had been watching the drama unfold on television. She began sobbing when she heard his voice. "I'm okay," he told her. "We don't know how many more planes might be trying to attack us. If anything else happens, take the children [son Michael, 8, and daughter Rachele, 15] and go to your brother's in Pennsylvania. I'll be here for a long time, maybe days. I'll call you later."

Fran uttered the same words she always said to him every time he left for work: "Make sure you come home."

Seconds after Kosowski exited the building, he heard a thunderous roar. At first he thought it was another plane, but the noise was different and a hundred times louder than any jet engine. The ground vibrated so much that he lost his balance and fell backward. Then he heard deafening booms in rapid-fire succession. Lying on his back, he looked up and couldn't believe his eyes. From the top of the South Tower down, each floor was pancaking onto the floor below.

He scrambled to his feet and sprinted toward the WFC, but he couldn't run in a straight line because the ground was moving. On the way, he saw that an EMT who had fallen was having trouble getting up. Kosowski grabbed his arm, pulled him up, and said, "Come with me!"

Holding on to each other, they reached the WFC's double doors. Suddenly, a rush of air compressed from the collapsing South Tower whipped into the entranceway, shattering the glass. It picked up the two men, flung them about ten feet, and slammed them against a wall. Bruised, they got up off the floor and staggered toward the security area where the civilians, security guards, and Parrino were clustered.

Parrino asked Kosowski, "What's going on?"

"The South Tower, it just collapsed!"

"That's impossible. Something bad must have happened, but not that."

The EMT came over and confirmed what Kosowski had stated. "It's true," said the EMT. "The entire building came down."

The civilians in the room gasped, and a few of them began to cry. "Oh, God, what do we do now?"

Parrino and Kosowski shepherded everyone to the back of the security area and looked for an escape route. A guard tried opening the metal doors at four different exits, but they were sealed shut because the building had gone into an automatic emergency lockdown.

"We'll find a way out," Parrino announced to the group. "We're going to stick together and remain calm." Staying composed was getting harder to do for some, because smoke and dust were pouring into the smashed doors and broken windows of the entrance. With help from the guards, Parrino began ripping towels and extra uniform shirts and passing out the strips of fabric to each person to use as masks against the thick, blinding dust.

As they searched for another way out, they passed through the security room, where a dozen monitors displayed video from closed-circuit cameras throughout the building. Kosowski pointed to two monitors with black screens and asked the guard, "What do these security cameras cover?"

"West Street."

"Are they broken?" Kosowski asked.

"No, they're working. That's what's out there right now—nothing but darkness."

"We need to get out of here," said Parrino. "Another plane could be heading this way, maybe to take out the World Financial Center."

"We can't get out through the other exits," said Kosowski. "So let's go into the worst part of the building and see if we can escape through the front."

"But that's where all the dust and soot are coming from," said Parrino.

"I know. But I think it's the only way out."

One of the guards broke into a locker and handed flashlights to the two officers.

With Kosowski leading the way through the blurry black haze, they lurched into the destroyed lobby. They shoved aside the debris until they had created an opening wide enough for them to get out.

As they emerged from the building, Kosowski yelped in pain. He had struck his leg against a glowing hot piece of metal. There was nothing he could do except shrug off the injury.

Parrino peered through the ground-hugging dust cloud that had turned from black to a gloomy gray. Seeing nothing but devastation outside, he said, "This isn't the place where we came in."

"Yeah, it is," Kosowski replied.

"But, Mike, the South Tower isn't here."

"Roger, I told you earlier. The building fell. It's gone."

After summoning the rest of the people who were inside, the two escorted them over and around the rubble toward West and Vesey Streets. On the way, they found two injured firefighters. One was lying down with back and neck injuries, and the other was slumped against the wall, holding his chest.

While Kosowski comforted the firefighters, he told the people who had been following him, "The North Tower could be the next to come down, so you must get away from here. Go north or take the bridges, just as long as you move far from here. Now go!"

He stayed with the injured men until several firefighters arrived and carried them to a waiting ambulance. Parrino returned to the security office because it was one of the few places with a phone line that still worked. He needed to stay in touch with police headquarters.

At West and Vesey Streets, Kosowski met up with Captain Winski, who told him they needed to get to a temporary police headquarters several blocks northwest of Ground Zero. As the two hurried west on Vesey Street, Kosowski stumbled and fell flat on his face. Picking himself up, he discovered that he had tripped over the legs of a woman who was trying to hide under an SUV. Only half her body was underneath the vehicle; her legs extended out in the street.

Hearing her cry, he kneeled down and asked, "Are you hurt?"

"No, I'm all right," she replied while still sobbing.

"You have to get out from under there, sweetheart. This isn't a good place to be."

"No. I want to stay here. I'm okay, honest I am."

Kosowski refused to take no for an answer. "You really must leave. The danger isn't over yet." He gently reached for her hand and coaxed her out. He could see the terror in the makeup-smeared face of the twentysomething woman. "Come with me," he said in a comforting voice. "I'll make sure you're safe."

He escorted the trembling woman to two nearby female EMTs, who cleaned the dusty gunk out of her and Kosowski's eyes before leading her away. By now, people west of the WFC were rushing north on North End Avenue. Many were in full panic mode, some falling down. He darted here and there to help them to their feet and encouraged them to move rapidly but safely out of the area.

When his pager beeped, indicating he needed to call police headquarters, he tried his cell phone but couldn't get a signal. So he went into a construction trailer near the corner of North End Avenue and Murray Street to make his call.

After he finished, he stepped outside. For the second time in less than 30 minutes, he heard horrendous rumbling and incredibly loud booms. He looked to the southeast and saw the North Tower crumbling. "Oh no! Not again!" he said out loud.

He began hollering to people nearby, "Get in the trailer! Get in the trailer!" He flung open the door and motioned for those within earshot to run inside. "Come in here! Hurry up!" Twenty . . . then fifty . . . then eighty people crammed into the trailer as debris began pounding the roof. He kept the door open, pulling even more people into the cramped space. When there was absolutely no way to squeeze another body inside, he closed the door.

As the huge black cloud of dust and ash shrouded the trailer, the unlucky people who were still outside banged on the door, begging to be let inside. "There's no more room!" shouted Kosowski. "I'm sorry." In desperation, they ripped the siding off the bottom of the trailer and crawled underneath to escape the dust cloud and falling debris.

Inside, a man in the middle of the jam-packed trailer panicked and screamed, "We're going to die!"

"No, we're safe," Kosowski said reassuringly. "Stay calm and everything will be fine. We just have to wait it out."

Once the dust cloud lightened up, he opened the door and steered everyone out, with instructions to proceed north.

Figuring the worst was over, he went looking for his partners, Joe Cosaluzzo and Hugh McGough. He hoped they hadn't been caught near the North Tower when it fell. During his search, he was struck by the number of people, many covered in gray dust, walking around aimlessly as if they were in a suspended state of animation. They reminded him of zombies.

When Kosowski got his first close-up glimpse of the ruins of the two towers, he was astounded. "It's like a war zone," he muttered to himself. He refused to even think about how high the death toll could be.

Early in the afternoon, he reunited with Cosaluzzo and McGough, whose clothes, like his, were covered in gray powder. "We thought you were dead," said Cosaluzzo. Added McGough, "You're on the list of the missing. Man, are we glad you're alive."

"I am, too. I was lucky. It's a great feeling to see that you both weren't hurt. Where were you when the towers came down?"

"We were evacuating people from buildings in the area," McGough answered.

"We all survived, and we helped many others survive, too," said Kosowski. "At least something went right on this awful day."

For weeks after the 9/11 attacks, Detective Sergeant Mike Kosowski searched the debris field. He worked even though he suffered the pain of three herniated discs in his neck and two in his back, caused by being thrown against the wall during the South Tower collapse.

"The whole first month, I kept asking myself, 'Did this really happen?'" he recalls. "Every day was the same, digging and poking around in the rubble and breathing all that toxic air. It was like the movie Groundhog Day, only there was nothing funny about it. I was working down there in twelve-hour shifts and sleeping in the dorm at the police precinct."

Kosowski was later assigned to the dump on Staten Island where all the debris was taken. His job was to sift through the junk and remnants for human remains and personal items such as purses, cell phones, and billfolds. He gave whatever he found to a team that tried to identify the remains or determine the owners of the items, which were then turned over to the victims' loved ones.

Like thousands of others who worked the pile, Kosowski developed induced asthma and other serious ailments caused by breathing the poisonous air at Ground Zero. After serving 21 years on the force and receiving the Medal of Valor for his actions on 9/11, he retired in January 2004.

Out of boredom, he began studying poker and playing it online. In 2009, he placed high enough in a 16,000-player online contest that he was invited to play in a face-to-face televised tournament against three other amateur card players. The winner would get the chance to play for $1 million against Daniel Negreanu, one of the world's top professional poker players.

Kosowski beat his fellow amateurs and then squared off against Negreanu on the TV show PokerStars.net Million Dollar Challenge. The retired sergeant had read all of Negreanu's books and watched how he played in previously televised games. So Kosowski felt prepared. Relying on a combination of good cards and his ability to recognize a bluff (a skill he learned on the police force), Kosowski beat the pro and won the $1 million jackpot.

"I consider myself an exceptionally lucky man," says Kosowski, who donated a portion of his winnings to the Family of Freedoms Scholarship Fund for the children of victims of 9/11 and to City Harvest, a charity that helps feed the homeless and needy of New York City. "I was lucky on 9/11. I only wish that more people on that day could have been as lucky."

"If You Die Here, We All Die Here"

CHARLES "CHUCK" SEREIKA
Paramedic

It's shortly before 10 A.M. Five Port Authority cops, loaded with safety and rescue gear, are rushing through an underground concourse between the two towers, determined to save lives.

Sergeant John McLoughlin, 46, a 21-year veteran, leads his men—Officers Will Jimeno, 33; Dominick Pezzulo, 36; Christopher Amoroso, 29; and Antonio Rodrigues, 35. Suddenly, they hear rhythmic booms and intense rumbles. Then the ceiling opens up, and the five are buried under broken concrete and steel. They don't realize that the South Tower is collapsing.

Amoroso and Rodrigues are killed instantly. Jimeno is pinned at a 45-degree angle by a concrete wall that has tumbled onto his lap. McLoughlin lies 20 feet away trapped in a coffin-sized crevice. Pezzulo, the strongest of the group, squirms free from the debris in a small triangle-shaped chamber. He tries again and again to lift the wall off Jimeno, but it's too heavy.

Then the survivors are bombarded with even more falling rubble, this time from the collapse of the North Tower. A large slab of concrete slams into Pezzulo, knocking him to the floor. Crying out in pain, he moans, "Willie, I'm hurt bad."

Jimeno tries to keep him alert, talking to him about life, family, and work. Soon, though, Pezzulo's voice gets weaker. They both know he's dying. "Willie, don't forget I died trying to save you guys."

"Dominick, I'll never forget."

Pezzulo raises his arm and points his service pistol toward a slender shaft of sunlight coming through a hole 30 feet above them. He fires a shot at the hole in an attempt to alert rescuers to the survivors' location. Then his arm goes limp, and his head slumps. Jimeno watches in gut-wrenching despair as his buddy takes his final breath.

Staring at the hole, Jimeno waits for someone to appear. But one long, unbearable hour drags into the next without any sign of rescue.

Although he and McLoughlin can't see each other because of the rubble between them, they carry on a conversation. McLoughlin says he's in pain and that his legs are crushed. He can't get anything on his radio except static. The two try to boost each other's spirits and take turns yelling for help. Eventually the light from above *begins to fade to dusk. Jimeno and McLoughlin, who have been drifting in and out of consciousness all day, finally come to terms with their grim predicament.*

They are prepared to die.

Chuck Sereika had slipped into a deep funk. He had been holed up in his New York City apartment for five days, not answering the phone, not showering, not shaving, not doing anything but moping.

For years he had been battling depression, alcoholism, and an eating disorder and was still haunted by memories of an abusive childhood. His problems had cost him jobs and friends and forced him into recent stays at rehabilitation centers in Arizona and New Mexico. The 32-year-old man had been back in the city for two months, and although he remained sober, he couldn't overcome his melancholy. He just wanted to be alone.

On September 11, Sereika was awakened by the shrieks of sirens. Living on busy 57th Street, he was used to hearing emergency vehicles, but not as many as there were this morning. Yawning, he shuffled over to his computer, clicked on his e-mail, and read several messages — including some from strangers in Europe — that left him befuddled. They were saying things like "Hope New York is okay," "Our hearts are with you," and "Be careful."

Something bad must have happened, he thought. He turned on the TV and jerked wide awake when he learned that terrorists had attacked the World Trade Center. He watched in shock at the ghastly replays of the Twin Towers' death from all different angles.

Shaken by this atrocity, Sereika listened to the voice messages on his cell phone that he'd been ignoring. The most recent one was from his sister, Joy Sereika-Copulos, who had called about an hour earlier. He always had a rocky relationship with her, as he did with other members of his family. But he and Joy had been trying to patch things up in recent weeks. That's why he was touched by her message: "I know you're down there helping. I hope you'll be okay. I love you."

Gee, she thinks I'm at the World Trade Center, he thought. *Maybe I should go down there and do something useful—something I haven't done in a long time.* He showered and shaved and then went to his closet where he kept his old uniform. He hadn't worn it in over two years, not since his problems caused him to quit the work he loved—being a paramedic. For 15 years, he had treated victims of accidents and heart attacks and muggings throughout the New York metropolitan area.

He put on a New York State paramedic sweatshirt, blue pants, work boots, and a badge, the typical attire that he wore at his last job in emergency medical care. *Maybe I can help bandage victims or splint some broken limbs. I just hope nobody asks to see my certification.* He had let it expire. From a strictly legal standpoint, he was going to impersonate a certified paramedic. He reasoned, *Even though I don't have my certification, I still have the knowledge and training I need to treat victims.*

At nearby St. Luke's-Roosevelt Hospital Center, he joined three nurses, a retired NYPD detective, and a volunteer firefighter from Long Island, who were waiting for a ride in an FDNY ambulance toward the site. When Sereika got into the vehicle, one of the ambulance's paramedics grew suspicious and asked him to change out the regulator on a portable oxygen tank. Sereika performed the task easily. "Is there anything else you want me to do?" he asked, knowing the skeptical paramedic was testing him. The paramedic shook his head.

During the ride, Sereika thought, *There might be hundreds, maybe thousands, of people who are hurt. All my training is going to be put to the test.*

When they arrived at an aid station a few blocks north of the WTC late in the morning, he was stunned by the ash, dust, and paper that had blanketed the streets. *Wow, it looks like a snowstorm in September, only gray instead of white.* Firefighters were lugging casualties in body bags, flames were licking out of shattered windows of other WTC buildings, and heavy equipment rumbled toward the ruins.

He, like many of the paramedics, EMTs, nurses, and doctors, spent much of the day waiting to treat the injured. But by this time, there were hardly any. Thinking he might be useful elsewhere, he walked to the debris field, where he noticed most of the firefighters and police officers were standing off to the side, looking traumatized, depressed, and helpless. They had been ordered to keep off the pile, which meant they couldn't search for, much less rescue, possible survivors. The area was deemed too dangerous because of shifting rubble and fears that other burning buildings in the complex would collapse. The blazing 47-story 7 WTC on Vesey Street had collapsed less than an hour earlier. Despite the hazards, several construction workers and civilians were ignoring the orders and searching on their own.

I should go on the pile, Sereika thought. *I can't let Joy down.* He closed his eyes and prayed, *God, guide me so I can help someone in your name.* Over the previous weeks, he had found strength in prayer, especially in his quest to stay sober and overcome his problems.

Without any sense of fear, he climbed onto the unstable, smoldering pile. The thick dust on the rubble made everything slick. One false step could send him plunging into a 50-foot-deep fiery gap. Walking carefully on all fours, he peered into crevasses and voids, hollering, "Can anyone hear me? Hello? Anybody in there?" When he didn't get a response, he moved on to the next hole.

As he crawled over the tangled steel and crumbled concrete, he became overwhelmed with sadness. He felt he was walking on hallowed ground, an unexpected cemetery for hundreds upon hundreds of innocent people who were dead beneath his feet. *God, let me see only what I need to see and nothing else.* He was afraid that if he saw too many gruesome things, he would leave for good.

After scouring the outer edges of the pile for about

an hour, he stepped off for a water break and wondered if he should risk further searching. *I'm not paid to be here. I'm not expected to be here except that Joy thinks I'm helping. Well, I've been on the pile, and I've tried to find survivors without any luck, so maybe I should go.*

But then a picture crept into his mind of a woman and child trapped under the rubble. He couldn't tell if it was his imagination or some divine image, but either way he felt compelled to continue his search. *God, lead me to do some good,* he prayed.

As he headed back to the pile, he noticed a man in a panel truck who had convinced police to let him through. The man was offering free flashlights to searchers. "Can I have one?" Sereika asked him.

"Here, take four of them," the man replied, thrusting the flashlights into Sereika's hands.

By now it was dusk. Through the smoke, he saw few searchers, because most had been shooed away by officials for their own safety. He didn't care. As gaps in the ruins glowed from the flames below, he climbed onto the pile and carefully worked his way toward the middle. Debris was still shifting, and the smoky haze made crawling on it more hazardous than ever. For the first time, Sereika was feeling scared. More than once he thought of turning around, but he kept telling himself, *I must go on. I can't let God down, or Joy, or anyone who might need my help.*

At the center of the pile, he spotted a Marine dressed

in camouflage and web gear motioning for him to come over.

The Marine was David Karnes, who had spent 23 years in the Marine Corps infantry and was now a senior accountant at the firm Deloitte Touche in Wilton, Connecticut. When the WTC was attacked, Karnes told his colleagues, "We're at war." He left work, got a military haircut, and went home to put on the pressed and starched Marine fatigues that he kept in his closet. He gathered his gear—rope, canteen, KA-BAR knife, and flashlight. Next, he went to church and asked his pastor to say a prayer for him. Then he drove to Ground Zero and, because of his uniform and military bearing, he gained access to the site and began searching. He would shout, "United States Marines! If you can hear me, yell or tap!" After about an hour of silence, he heard a muffled voice coming from inside a void. Someone below was shouting "Eight-Thirteen! Eight-Thirteen!" That was Port Authority Police Department code for officer in need of assistance.

"Someone's trapped down there!" Karnes shouted to Sereika, pointing at a hole by his feet.

When Sereika scrambled over to the spot, Karnes led him ten feet into the gap where he shouted down to the survivor, "Where are you?"

"Help me!" a voice called back.

The two searchers wiggled a few more feet into the void, but still couldn't see anything. "Wave your hand!" Karnes yelled. They pointed their flashlights back and forth in the darkness until Sereika declared, "I see it! I see a hand sticking out of the rubble about another fifteen feet down."

Karnes and Sereika looked at each other. They were both thinking the same thing: It was incredibly dangerous to go much deeper. The debris was completely insecure, and any little shift could cause a cave-in, trapping or killing any rescuer.

"Don't leave!" the voice pleaded.

"Don't worry," Sereika replied. "We won't." He took a deep breath and thought, *My life isn't worth any more than whoever is down there, so . . .* Turning to Karnes, he shrugged and said, "Let me see if I can reach him."

Even though he had no gear or any kind of training for this type of rescue, the former paramedic wormed his way down around broken rebar and concrete slabs as whiffs of acrid smoke stung his eyes and nose. Every time he jostled a piece of debris, he was showered with dust and small chunks of rubble.

I don't know what I'm doing. I'm probably not going to get out of here alive. At least I should call Joy and tell her good-bye. He pulled his cell phone out of his pocket, but it slipped out of his hand and tumbled through a crack, lost forever.

He kept going deeper until he came to another void that, from the beam of his flashlight, looked to go down another 50 feet. He shuddered because he was afraid of heights. *That must be an elevator shaft,* he thought.

"Over here!" The voice was a few feet from the shaft.

Sereika moved toward the sound and crawled into a tiny space where he found a man trapped up to his chest in rubble. He was wearing the uniform of the PAPD. *Oh, great, he's a cop,* Sereika thought. *I'm going to be in big trouble if anyone finds out that I'm not a licensed paramedic anymore. Oh well, I can't leave now.*

"Hi, I'm Chuck. I'm a paramedic from Westchester. What's your name?"

"Will Jimeno."

"Will, I'm going to help get you out of here, okay?" *How in the world am I going to do that?* "Are you in pain?"

"Yes, my legs. I can't move them, and it's hard to breathe, and I'm so thirsty."

Sereika turned on his extra flashlights and set them around the chamber so he could see. Then he felt Jimeno's wrist. *Good, his pulse is still strong.* He checked Jimeno's eyes and fingers. *He's alert and oriented, and blood circulation is good.* "Hey, Marine!" he yelled to Karnes. "This guy needs water."

Karnes moved farther into the hole until he was about five feet away and tossed his canteen to Sereika who gave it to Jimeno.

Unexpectedly, Jimeno began blabbering, "Sarge! Sarge! We're going to get out of here! A paramedic just showed up. Isn't that great, Sarge?"

Not hearing anyone else, Sereika assumed that Jimeno was talking perhaps to a dead sergeant. But then from a nearby but unseen tomb farther in the rubble,

Sereika heard a weak voice cry out, "Medic! Help me! Medic!"

My God. A desperate situation is now even more desperate. "Hey, Marine!" Sereika shouted to Karnes. "There's another survivor! He's buried deeper in another pocket, and I can't see him!"

"He's my sergeant, John McLoughlin," said Jimeno. "There were three others with us, but they're all dead."

"Medic!" McLoughlin moaned.

"After I free Will, I'll come for you," Sereika promised. "Help is on the way." *I wonder if anyone else will show up. Our best hope is to dig him out one piece at a time.*

Sereika didn't know that Karnes had tried calling for help on his cell phone, but couldn't get through to anyone in New York. So the ex-Marine called his sister—who coincidentally is also named Joy—in Pittsburgh and told her to call her police department in the hope they could find a way to reach NYPD and FDNY and tell them where the survivors were located.

Because parts of the chamber were narrow, Sereika had to balance himself on his right arm and reach with his left to pull out the mashed concrete and twisted metal bits one piece at a time—a task made more difficult by the fact that he was right-handed. With every piece of debris removed, the rubble in the cramped space creaked and groaned. Karnes tossed down his Marine-issue carbon-steel fighting-and-utility knife to help Sereika in his efforts to free Jimeno.

Meanwhile, McLoughlin, during the periodic times when he was conscious, kept calling out, "Medic! Medic! Medic! Help me!"

"We'll get to you as quickly as we can," Sereika assured him.

Smoke was slithering into the void, and the temperature was soaring way beyond anything Sereika had ever experienced before. As flames crept closer, he spotted Jimeno's gun—a nickel-plated Smith & Wesson. *I can't let the fire reach the bullets or they'll probably kill one of us.* He grabbed the pistol, emptied it of bullets, and threw them away from the flames. Then he tossed the gun up to Karnes.

About 30 minutes into the rescue attempt, Scott Strauss and Patrick "Paddy" McGee, officers from the NYPD's elite Emergency Services Unit, climbed into the void and positioned themselves behind Sereika. Their arrival caused mixed emotions in him. *Oh no, more cops. I'm in big trouble. But at least they're trained for this kind of rescue.* After the two introduced themselves, Strauss asked Sereika, "What's your name?"

"Charles."

"Okay, Chuck."

Then Strauss looked up at Karnes and asked, "What do I call you?"

Karnes replied, "Staff Sergeant Karnes."

"That's four syllables," Strauss said. "Is there anything shorter, because it's hard to talk in here with all this smoke."

"Okay, you can call me Staff Sergeant."

The former paramedic returned to removing the debris. With each piece of rubble that he pulled out, he handed it to Strauss, who gave it to McGee, who threw it down the elevator shaft. Everyone was drenched in sweat.

Firefighter Tommy Asher squeezed into the hole to hold off the flames as best he could. Because water hoses were being sliced by the sharp edges of debris, Asher had to use carbon dioxide cans to extinguish the fires in the chamber. Sometimes he snuffed out small patches of flames with his gloved hands.

At Sereika's request, Asher delivered an oxygen tank and an IV setup. Sereika hooked Jimeno to the IV and placed an oxygen mask over Jimeno's nose and mouth. Immediately, the officer began to breathe easier and color returned to his face.

McGee kept talking to McLoughlin, trying to keep him conscious. "Don't give up, Irish Eyes. We'll get to you as soon as we can free your partner." After one particularly long quiet spell, McGee hollered, "Irish eyes, Irish eyes, can you hear me?"

He's not answering, Sereika thought. *I think he's dead. We couldn't get to him in time. We let him down.*

Trying to hide their regret, Sereika, Strauss, and McGee worked even harder elbow to elbow in the cramped space, shoveling with their hands and pushing aside pieces of concrete. Karnes, meanwhile, was trying to make the entrance to the hole bigger.

Police and firefighters soon clustered around the top of the void to provide encouragement and whatever equipment and supplies were needed below. Asher delivered more IV bags for Jimeno. He also brought a self-contained breathing apparatus (SCBA) for the rescuers who were finding it increasingly hard to breathe in the boiling hot smoky chamber. Sereika, who kept working without a SCBA, was getting woozy and confused from lack of oxygen.

After sucking in air from the SCBA, Strauss told Sereika, "Here, breathe on this for a little while."

"I'm all right," mumbled Sereika.

"That's not a request, Chuck. That's an order."

Sereika did what he was told. After inhaling a few puffs from the SCBA, he became more clear-headed and continued his work.

Suddenly, they heard McLoughlin mutter, "Medic! Medic!"

That's a relief. He's not dead after all.

"Irish Eyes, you're back with the living!" said McGee. "Stay with us now."

The painstaking digging continued ever so slowly amid rescuers' fears of getting buried alive themselves. Sereika could hear rumbles, bangs, and crashes as parts of the debris field collapsed or shifted. At one point, firemen above hollered down, "Get out of there! The pile is unsafe!" Referring to the closest standing building in the WTC complex, they shouted, "Number four is burning like crazy and near collapse!"

Sereika's brain was telling him to scramble to safety. He could have left, and no one would have questioned it, because he had done more than anyone could ask for. But he wasn't going anywhere—at least not without Jimeno.

"Don't leave me," begged Jimeno, who was getting panicky. "Just cut my legs off and get me out of here!"

"Relax, Will," Sereika said. "We're not that desperate. Besides, I don't have any training for amputating limbs. We're staying here until the end—one way or the other. If you die here, we all die here. We're in this together. We're not going anywhere without you."

After he calmed down, Jimeno said, "My wife, Allison, is seven months pregnant. We're going to have a baby girl. Allison likes the name Olivia. I hadn't been so sure about the name. But now I think that's a good name, don't you?"

"Yes, it's a pretty name," Sereika replied.

"In case I die, I want my last thought to be of my wife and baby girl."

Is that the woman and child that came into my mind? Sereika thought. He looked Jimeno in the eyes and said, "Will, you're not going to die."

After Sereika got Jimeno's chest free, he saw that the cop's legs were trapped under rebar. A Sawzall, a battery-operated electric saw that can cut through steel, was lowered into the hole. "I need to protect Will from sparks and flying metal," said Sereika. "Tommy, give me your helmet and bunker coat." Asher took his gear off and handed it to him. Sereika covered Jimeno with the coat, put the oxygen mask over his face, and placed the helmet on top of that. Sereika, who had never used a Sawzall before, then sliced the rebar, hoping that the vibration wouldn't cause the void to collapse, or that the sparks and loud noise wouldn't further stress Jimeno.

After removing the cut rebar, Sereika discovered that a portion of a cement-block wall still pinned Jimeno's feet. Sereika cut the laces away from the cop's boots and tried to pull him out, but he didn't budge. Attempting to move the slab out of the way proved futile because it was just too heavy, and Sereika had no leverage.

Strauss then yelled up for a Hurst Tool known as the Jaws of Life, a hydraulic power tool that can lift or spread an obstruction to help free a trapped person. After it was lowered into the hole, Sereika, who was exhausted and not trained to use the heavy device, had trouble operating it. So he switched places with the more experienced Strauss.

The rescuers were aware that using the tool presented a significant danger. If the piece of cement block wall were moved, it could cause the entire chamber to collapse. But it was a chance they had to take.

"Will, one of two things will happen," Strauss told Jimeno. "One is it works, and we all get out of here. The other is that it doesn't work, and we all get buried. I'm betting it's going to work."

The void began creaking and groaning, sending a torrent of pulverized concrete onto the rescuers. The mortar started to split on the cinder block wall, but not enough to break apart.

"The tool has reached its limit," Strauss complained.

"I've got an idea," said Sereika. "Why don't I place rocks underneath it to give it more leverage?"

"It's worth a try," Strauss said.

Sereika crawled under Strauss and positioned the rocks so the Jaws of Life would have a better reach. Once again Strauss operated the tool. This time, with the extra leverage, it split the cinder-block wall and moved aside the last remaining obstruction.

"Will, you're free!" Sereika exclaimed. As he tried to untangle the IV lines from Jimeno's arm, Sereika called for firefighters to lower a Stokes basket. After it came down, he strapped in Jimeno and then, with great satisfaction, watched him get pulled up.

"I'm going to throw a big barbecue for all of you as soon as I get home," pledged Jimeno as he left the chamber that had held him for 13 agonizing hours.

"Great, I'll bring the steaks," Sereika said.

The former paramedic was exhausted. He had been cooped up in the confined smoky chamber for nearly four hours, digging relentlessly and administering the oxygen, water, and intravenous drips that kept Jimeno alive. His gloves had holes in every finger. His sweatshirt was ripped to shreds. He was having trouble breathing.

But now McLoughlin, who was barely alive and buried deeper in the void, needed to be rescued.

"My lungs are shot, and I'm hurt," Sereika told

Strauss. "I don't think I can do any more. I'm too wiped out."

"We all are," said Strauss. He radioed to his superiors, "We're spent. You need to bring in another crew."

Sereika didn't think he had the strength to climb out, but he managed. When he finally emerged from the hole at about 11 P.M., the tension of the last four hours melted away. *I never thought I'd get out of here alive.* An FDNY battalion chief patted him on the back and said, "Good job, son."

Gazing out over the ruins, which were lit by large portable construction lights, Sereika was startled to see hundreds of police officers, firefighters, and workers standing side by side. They had laid ladders from the hole all the way across the debris field to the ground. From hand to hand, they passed Jimeno, still securely strapped in the Stokes basket, to a waiting ambulance.

Then they helped Sereika, Strauss, McGee, and Karnes walk on the ladders across the rubble. Along the way, the rescuers were praised with comments like "Great job" and "Way to go."

When they stepped off the pile, they were told, "Go right if you need medical attention, left if you don't."

Everyone went to the right except Sereika. Even though he had difficulty breathing and was hurt all over, dehydrated, fatigued, and starving, he went to the left. He was still worried he would get in trouble if officials discovered he wasn't certified.

But no one knew who he was or where he came

from. No one knew his full name or address or phone number. No one knew anything about him, other than he was a paramedic named Chuck who never stopped working to free a trapped victim.

And that was just fine with him.

Shivering from the cool night air that had chilled his sweat-drenched body, Sereika wrapped his dust-covered arms around his torn blue sweatshirt. He stared one last time at the deadly pile that had buried so many innocent lives. Then the mysterious hero who had saved one of the last survivors of 9/11 walked off into the night.

It took a fresh team of rescue workers another eight hours to free PAPD Sergeant John McLoughlin. They brought him out about 7 A.M. the next day after he had been trapped for a harrowing 21 hours. He was so gravely injured that doctors kept him in a medically induced coma for six weeks. McLoughlin, who underwent 30 operations on his legs, spent four months in the hospital and rehabilitation clinic.

After being rescued, Officer Will Jimeno underwent eight surgeries in twelve days and spent nearly three months in the hospital and rehabilitation clinic. The highlight of his recovery was holding his infant daughter, Olivia Jimeno, who was born on November 26, 2001, on his thirty-fourth birthday.

McLoughlin and Jimeno were the last two cops pulled alive from the ruins of the WTC. On June 11, 2002, McLoughlin, using a walker, and Jimeno, walking with a limp, made their way across a stage at Madison Square Garden to receive the Port Authority's highest award—the Medal of Honor. Both retired from the force in 2004.

David Karnes, who had accompanied Jimeno to the hospital after the rescue, re-enlisted in the Marines at age 45. He told reporters he wanted "to go after the people who did this, so it never happens again." On his second tour of duty, he served in the combat zone in Iraq for 17 months.

After Jimeno was carried off the pile, Sereika left Ground Zero. "I was a huge mess physically and mentally," he recalls. "I walked a few blocks and stopped in a Subway shop to buy a sandwich and a drink. People stared at me funny because I was covered in dust and my sweatshirt was all torn. I walked on the abandoned streets for about a mile to my cousin Jennifer Sklias-Gahan's flat in Greenwich Village. I was shivering and had trouble breathing, and she took care of me that night. I told Jennifer what had happened, and she believed me." But other family members didn't believe him.

"I understand why my family doubted the story," Sereika says. "Heck, it was hard for me to believe it—and I was there. I decided not to talk about it anymore."

Seven weeks later, on October 30, 2001, the New York Times published a story about the rescue. The article referred to "a paramedic, known only by his first name, Chuck" and described how he was instrumental in saving Jimeno's life. Sereika's cousin Robert Soukeras, a special agent for the Department of Alcohol, Tobacco, Firearms and Explosives, read the story and immediately called Sereika.

Sereika contacted reporter Jim Dwyer, identified himself as Chuck the paramedic, and asked to be put in touch with Jimeno. Because several people had claimed to be the mysterious paramedic, Dwyer asked Sereika questions that only someone involved in the rescue would know. After Sereika answered them, Dwyer told him, "You're the real deal." The reporter then wrote a follow-up story the next week, revealing Sereika's identity.

Sereika visited Jimeno, who was still recovering in the hospital. "It felt really good to see him and have the chance to wish him well," Sereika recalls. "We are all really lucky, because we could easily have died down there."

Adds Sereika, who is sober and co-owns a successful cleaning business in Vero Beach, Florida, "Me, a hero? No way. I'm not the type. I believe I was there for a reason. Will was not supposed to die.

"All the real heroes died that day. The rest of us just did what we could."

THE PENTAGON

The Pentagon, headquarters of the United States Department of Defense, is named after the word for a five-sided geometric shape. The immense five-story-tall building, located in Arlington County, Virginia, is considered one of the most secure structures in the country.

As the world's largest office building by floor area, it has 6.5 million square feet, or 28.7 acres, under its roof, which is three times the floor space of the Empire State Building. It's the work place for 26,000 military and civilian employees, and is so big that it has six zip codes.

The Pentagon's unique design features office space in five concentric rings that encircle a five-acre outdoor pentagon-shaped central courtyard. These rings are lettered A through E, with the A Ring being the closest to the courtyard and the E Ring being the farthest away. The offices in the E Ring are the only ones with outside views and are generally occupied by senior officials. Radiating out from the courtyard, like spokes on a bicycle, are ten numbered corridors that intersect all the rings. Even though there are 17.5 miles of corridors, it takes only seven minutes to walk between any two points in the building.

Ironically, ground was broken for construction of the Pentagon on September 11, 1941—exactly 60 years to the day before it was attacked.

On September 11, 2001, a jetliner hijacked by terrorists plowed into the west side of the building between Corridor 4 and 5. Military personnel and civilians braved fire, smoke, and fumes to rescue friends and coworkers.

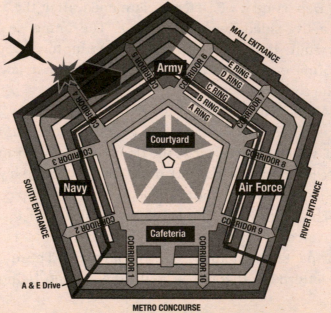

"I'm Not Giving Up"

COLONEL PHILIP MCNAIR

United States Army

American Airlines Flight 77—a hijacked jetliner with 64 people aboard, including five terrorists—slammed into the west side of the Pentagon about 14 feet above the ground at a speed of 530 miles per hour.

At the moment of impact, a fireball twice the height of the building roared through the roof and out in every direction. As the belly of the plane penetrated the first floor, fuel exploded in a blast that sent shock waves hurtling down hallways. A super-heated tidal wave of fiery debris raced through office space, air vents, and stairwells almost at the speed of sound.

By the time the plane came to a halt in less than one second, it had plowed 310 feet into the Pentagon, destroying everything in its path and buckling sections of the second floor. It knocked down more than

30 steel-reinforced concrete columns and severely damaged 20 more. The plane, its wings sheared off at impact, carved a huge trail of destruction through the E, D, and C Rings, wiping out the Army's Budget Office, the Navy Command Center, and the Defense Intelligence Agency, and wrecking many other offices.

And it all happened directly underneath the feet of Colonel Philip McNair.

At 9 A.M. that morning, McNair began conducting a meeting with 11 others in the windowless conference room of the Army's Office of Personnel on the second floor. They were unaware that the World Trade Center had been attacked minutes earlier.

At 9:37 A.M., Lieutenant Colonel Marilyn Wills was giving her report at the meeting when they heard a tremendous explosion and felt a concussion that nearly knocked them out of their chairs. The floor shook and the walls fractured as an orange fireball flew over their heads. *Did a bomb go off outside in the hallway?* McNair wondered. He looked up and saw the tiles in the ceiling rippling across the room with flames flashing above them. The ceiling burst into thousands of little pieces, and the lights went out. Then the room filled with acrid smoke, blackening out the battery-operated emergency lights in the upper corners.

Everyone was so stunned that it took a few seconds before they started to react. Still trying to understand what had happened, McNair told the group, "We need to get out of here as quickly as we can."

Smoke was sinking toward the floor, prompting someone to yell, "Get down and crawl so you can get below the smoke!"

Lieutenant Colonel Robert Grunewald leaped across the conference table toward McNair's executive assistant, Martha Carden, who was curled up on the floor, frozen in shock. "Martha, I'll get you!" he shouted.

Spending 25 years in the military, many of them in leadership positions, McNair assumed the mantle of responsibility. As the ranking officer for this group, he felt a duty to lead everyone to safety. *Make sure they get out,* he told himself. *Just worry about them rather than focus on yourself.* He had jumped out of airplanes and rappelled from helicopters, so he had faced danger before, although nothing like this.

The conference room had two doors. Someone tried to open the door that led into the E-Ring corridor, which was between the conference room and the executive offices. But that was jammed because the force from the explosion had twisted its frame.

Dropping to their hands and knees bought everyone a few precious seconds of breathable air under the thick smoke. At McNair's urging, they crawled in a line with each person holding on to the foot of the colleague in front. Then he led them out through the other door. It opened into a small interior room and out to the main office area—a huge space where 240 people worked in executive offices and in dozens of cubicles. The best offices in the department had windows that looked directly over the helipad. McNair used to watch President George W. Bush arrive in his helicopter. But on this day, the helipad had served as a target for the terrorists in the cockpit of the hijacked jetliner to aim for.

After everyone crawled out of the conference room, Lieutenant Colonel Dennis Johnson and Major Stephen Long broke off and went in a different direction. Grunewald and Carden also separated from the group.

Grasping and groping in the dark, people began to feel their way in the massive room. Remarkably, hardly anyone panicked. McNair heard someone in the darkness praying, "Our Father, who art in heaven . . ." Somewhere he heard voices calling out, "Over here!" and "Follow me!"

In the billowing smoke, McNair could see only about three feet ahead, making it difficult to find his way around the cubicles, desks, and copiers. Compounding the problem, everyone was unfamiliar with the layout, because they had recently moved in to that section after it had been renovated. With his head close to the floor, McNair felt he was crawling in a maze. *This is extremely confusing,* he told himself. *But I have to find a way. Others are depending on me to guide them out.*

Conditions were getting worse by the second. The fumes, which smelled like a toxic mix of jet fuel, melted plastic, and scorched wiring, seared McNair's throat.

He eventually crawled to a copy machine, which he recognized as the one nearest a door to the E-Ring corridor. "I think I found the way out," he told the group. But hopes of a quick escape were dashed when he saw flames licking under the door. He touched the door and jerked his hand away because it was so hot. "We can't go out this way," he said. "There's fire on the other side. We have to turn around."

They reversed themselves and headed back into the interior and away from their hoped-for exit. Once again they found themselves in the main area as flames and smoke spewed through gaps in the floor and the ceiling, turning the office into an unbearable oven. Amid the crackling sounds of fire, everyone could hear the annoying fire alarms and an automated voice system repeating over and over, "A fire emergency has been determined. Please evacuate. . . . A fire emergency has been determined. Please evacuate. . . ."

With McNair now in the back of the human daisy chain, they crawled in confusion toward dead ends or doors that wouldn't open. McNair peeled off from the group, because he thought he knew of a door they could use. But it turned out to be a locked supply closet. For the first time, he was beginning to wonder if they would make it out safely. It was getting harder to get air and easier to get discouraged. *This would be a really bad place to end my life, curled up next to an office-supply door.* He shook that thought from his mind. *I'm not giving up. I need to stay focused.*

Pushing chairs and tables out of the way while still on his hands and knees, McNair found some of his colleagues. Although he could hear people crying and moaning in other parts of the office, he and those in his group remained composed. They were determined to escape from the blinding smoke and choking fumes. But because no one knew where the source of the fire was or what had happened, finding a way out was still a matter of guesswork and luck.

Betty Maxfield, a civilian who worked for the army, crawled over to McNair and grabbed his ankle. "Don't let go," he told her. They were getting pelted by falling pieces of burning ceiling and melting plastic. The sprinkler system provided some relief from the intolerable heat. Water from the sprinklers not only soaked them but also formed dirty puddles on the carpet, which he scooped up and splashed on his face. .

Marilyn Wills took off her sweater and dunked it in one of the puddles to turn it into a makeshift filter. After she took a few breaths of fresher air through her sweater, she passed it back along the line so that everyone could take turns breathing through it.

The chain had been snaking along the floor in the smoky darkness for five minutes when someone in another part of the office yelled, "There's a window!" As the group crawled toward the voice, McNair began to see a dim glow through the smoke that brightened as they drew closer.

They finally reached a newly replaced window on the east side of the office that overlooked A&E Drive, a service road between the C and B Rings. During the

Pentagon renovations, old windows had been replaced with thick blast-proof ones that didn't open. Army Specialist Mike Petrovich picked up a printer and threw it against the window, but the machine bounced off the glass and hit him in the head.

Seeing that, some members of the group worried that they were doomed. They had made it this far and were only two inches of glass away from safety. But the glass was unbreakable.

Luckily, the impact from the plane had nudged the glass a few inches off the frame, allowing fresh air to seep in. One by one, McNair helped people in his group stick their faces next to the opening so they could suck in clean air. When it was McNair's turn, he looked down outside and saw six men from the Pentagon staring at him and the others who were trapped on the second floor.

"We're going to go out through this window and drop down," McNair told his colleagues in a voice raspy from inhaling smoke.

"But how?" asked one. "The opening isn't big enough, and it's impossible to break the window."

"Here's how," McNair replied. He began kicking at the frame. So did Petrovich. Using all their leg power, the two worked feverishly to dislodge the window from the frame until they made a gap wide enough for a person to squeeze through.

"Marilyn and I are going to lower you as far as we can," McNair explained to the others. "But it's a fifteen-foot drop—high enough to break your leg if you don't land right. Don't worry, though, because there are people below who'll try and catch you."

On the service road, Craig Powell, a towering Navy SEAL, instructed the five men with him to form a human net. They gathered in a circle, extended their arms, and held on to the forearms of those on the opposite side of the circle.

McNair climbed onto the three-foot-high window-sill and chose longtime Army personnel employee Lois Stevens to go first, because she was having serious difficulty breathing. When she balked, McNair ordered, "Lois, get your fanny up on the sill."

McNair and Wills helped position Stevens, a petite woman, out the window. From below, Powell shouted, "Go! We'll catch you!"

Stevens released her grip from McNair and Wills and fell with her arms and legs together. However, seeing her plunge toward them, the men on the ground instinctively backed away, leaving it up to Powell to catch her by the hips and bring her hard but safely to the ground.

Next, another woman, much bigger than Stevens, dropped from the window and landed right on Powell. On impact, both of them tumbled to the ground in pain. Before Powell had a chance to get set for the next person, another woman jumped. He dove underneath her just in time to break her fall.

After nearly everyone in McNair's group had

escaped, he told Wills, "Okay, Marilyn, it's your turn. You have to get out."

"I don't want to leave yet. Marian [her boss Marian Serva] disappeared somewhere back there, and I need to find her. This is the army. You don't leave a soldier behind."

"I'll go back and try to find her," said McNair. He crawled into the smoke until he was thwarted by intense heat and flames. He repeatedly shouted Serva's name. Not hearing a reply, he called out, "Is anybody there?" *It's no use,* he thought. *I can't go in any farther. There's nothing more I can do.*

When McNair returned to the window, Wills asked, "Did you find her?"

He shook his head. She burst into tears and started to head for the wall of smoke until he stopped her. "You have to get out right now!" he stressed. "That's an order!"

The men below had pulled a Dumpster next to the wall and placed a ladder in it, but its top rung was still several feet beneath the window. So Powell climbed into the bin and had one of his comrades place the bottom of the ladder on his shoulders so that the top reached near the base of the window. McNair then lowered Wills onto the ladder. While Powell held it steady, Wills climbed down into the arms of the men below.

By the time McNair descended the ladder, all the people in his small group were nowhere to be seen. They had been taken to a triage area that had been set up in the open-air central courtyard.

Somewhat shell-shocked and dazed, McNair tried to clear his head. *I'm okay. I'm not hurt.* He spotted a group of military men who were running in and out of a smoking hole on the first floor of the exterior wall of the C Ring. Their clothes were tattered and charred, their faces caked in soot. *I'd better see how I can help.* He hurried over to them and learned that navy people were trapped inside a blazing room behind a large air-conditioning unit. Debris blocked an escape route.

He joined several rescuers who had set up a bucket brigade. The person who was farthest inside the building would grab a piece of rubble or an object, such as an office chair, that was in the way, and pass it back to the next person, who handed it down the line until the last person would toss it in the street. Before getting overcome with smoke, the person at the head would run out to catch some fresh air while the next in line would take over. McNair helped shove computers, equipment, and office partitions out of the way.

While clearing a path, he spotted an arm poking out of the rubble. With another rescuer, he pulled out a woman who had been buried in a mound of debris. Then he and his comrades helped free six more navy people.

The rescuers had no water to snuff out the flames or tools to dig with, so McNair ran out and searched frantically for any equipment they could use. After getting a fire extinguisher, he ducked back into the hole. He sprayed foam onto the flames where the smoke was the thickest, but the stream sizzled and evaporated on contact. By now he was no longer hearing any cries for help. *Either everyone is out, or those who aren't are dead,* he thought.

Like the other rescuers, he was driven out by the smoke and flames. Heading for another hole, McNair and the others were stopped by a Pentagon security officer, who told him, "You guys have to leave, because there are reports of another plane heading this way."

"Another plane?" McNair asked in bewilderment. "What do you mean?"

"A plane hit the Pentagon."

"But I thought it was a bomb."

"No, it was a passenger plane. Two more hit the World Trade Center in New York. Another is still in the air, and it looks like it's aiming for Washington." (McNair would learn later that the fourth plane was hijacked United Airlines Flight 93, which ultimately crashed in Pennsylvania.)

Stunned by the news, McNair wandered down the service road and into the courtyard where the Army personnel office's security officer John Yates was on a stretcher being loaded into an ambulance. Seeing that Yates was badly burned, McNair bent down to take his hand, but a piece of charred skin came off. McNair looked in his eyes and said, "It's going to be okay, John."

As his adrenaline wore off, McNair couldn't talk or breathe well. He went over to a medic, who put him in an ambulance and gave him an IV on the way to the hospital. "I feel bad that you're taking me when there must be survivors a lot worse off than me," he said.

When the ambulance arrived at the hospital, medical personnel lined up at the emergency entrance, prepared for the onslaught of victims that never materialized. McNair was treated for smoke inhalation—his blood had seven times the limit of carbon monoxide—and spent the rest of the day lying in bed with an oxygen mask.

Because he recovered quickly, his wife, Nancy, was allowed to bring him home later that night. The next day he, like most everyone else in his department who was physically able, returned to the job but in temporary offices in Alexandria. "We're not going to let the terrorists interrupt our work," McNair explained to Nancy.

Whenever he went to work before 9/11, he always wore his Class B uniform—green trousers with a stripe down the side, a light gray-green shirt with an eagle insignia on each shoulder board and a name tag on his chest, and spit-shined shoes.

But on September 12, McNair showed up for work wearing his battle dress uniform—camouflage fatigues and boots. So did everyone else at the Army Personnel Command.

It was because the United States was now at war.

At 10:10 A.M., 27 minutes after American Airlines Flight 77 struck the Pentagon, the section of the building holding the second-floor personnel offices collapsed. It would take firefighters days to put out the fire.

The Army Personnel Directorate lost 24 of its 240 staff members.

"Who lived and who died came down to timing and circumstance—better for some, not so for others," McNair says.

One of his colleagues, Max Beilke, a retired master sergeant who worked in the retirement-services division, left the conference room at 9:30 A.M.—seven minutes before the attack—to attend another meeting in the executive office of McNair's boss, Lieutenant General Timothy Maude, the Army's deputy chief of staff for personnel. Sergeant Major Larry Strickland, who had been due to retire a month later, was supposed to have had the day off, but came in to attend that same meeting. The three were killed instantly. Beilke had been the last American soldier to leave Vietnam in 1975 when he was plucked off the roof of the U.S. Embassy in Saigon. General Maude was the highest-ranking officer at the Pentagon to die on September 11.

"If it had happened on any other day of the week, I would have been killed," McNair points out. "I would have been sitting at my desk, which was in the area that was completely destroyed—right outside the general's office—and where everybody in our department including secretaries, aides, and officers were killed.

"My meeting started at 9 A.M. in the conference room

across the hall and down a couple of doors. We were only sixty feet away from my desk."

Of the 11 people who were in the conference room when the plane hit, two never reached safety: Lieutenant Colonel Dennis Johnson and Major Steve Long. According to evidence found by firefighters, the pair tried to rescue others nearby rather than flee the fire. Long, a decorated combat veteran who worked in Alexandria, was at the Pentagon on that day only to attend McNair's meeting.

It took about six weeks before the Army Personnel Directorate moved back into the Pentagon. "We took pride that our operations weren't interrupted," McNair says. "Some never returned to the Pentagon. They just couldn't do it. For those of us who came back to the office, it was nonstop talk about the attack—where were you when it hit, how did you escape, did you see so-and-so. Later it occurred to me that those who talked about it at work fared better emotionally than those who didn't come back and were by themselves at home or in a hospital."

McNair was awarded the Soldier's Medal for putting his own life at risk to help save others on 9/11. "The Soldier's Medal to me confirms I did the right thing," he says. "When I escaped the fire, I was still capable of helping others. So that's what I did. I have a hard time thinking of myself as someone special. I'm not a hero. I'd like to think that most people would do what I did if they were in the same situation. It was just the right thing to do."

When McNair, the married father of two, retired in

2002, he was given the army's highest award for military service, the Distinguished Service Medal. He then went to work for the American Military University, which is part of the American Public University System, the largest provider of online higher education for military personnel. He is now vice president of academic services.

Even though years have passed since 9/11, McNair admits, "I think about it to some degree every single day."

"It's Us or Nobody"

LIEUTENANT COMMANDER
DAVID A. TARANTINO, JR.
CAPTAIN DAVID M. THOMAS, JR.
United States Navy

When American Airlines Flight 77 struck the Pentagon, Navy Captain David M. Thomas, Jr., thought the building had been rocked by an explosion. So he did what any navy person was trained to do—run toward the blast.

Thomas, 43, who had spent 12 years at sea, including as skipper of the destroyer USS *Ross* for 20 months, had been at his desk in the office of the Chief of Naval Operations on the third floor of C Ring. He was two corridors away from the airliner's impact point.

After countless damage-control drills, a sailor's instinct is to confront a disaster, not move away from it. After all, there are no fire departments aboard ship. It's fight the fire, protect your shipmates, and save your ship . . . or sink. So when Thomas felt the powerful shudder that fateful morning, he sprinted out of the corridor, down the stairways, and outside onto A&E Drive, the open-air service road between the B and C Rings. There, he saw plumes of smoke belching from two holes in a wall blown out by wreckage of the plane in a section of the Pentagon that housed the Navy Command Center.

My God, that's where Bob works! Thomas thought. Captain Robert "Bob" Dolan, former commander of the destroyer USS *John Hancock,* had been like a brother to Thomas since their days rooming together at the Naval Academy in Annapolis. Dolan had been the best man at Thomas's wedding and godfather to one of his kids. To Thomas, no one outside the immediate family was more important to him than "Doles," as he affectionately called him. *I've got to find Doles!*

At 9:38 A.M., Lieutenant Commander David A. Tarantino, Jr., felt a violent jolt in his office. He knew instantly that the Pentagon had been attacked, having watched on TV the horror unfolding in New York.

The 35-year-old navy physician bolted from his desk in the Office of Peacekeeping and Humanitarian Affairs on the fourth floor of the A Ring. The office was far enough away from the impact to escape serious damage. But everyone was ordered to evacuate immediately.

Tarantino, looking to use his medical skills, began searching for injured people in the hallway. It was getting crowded with bleeding, coughing workers who didn't know where to go, because smoke had concealed the exit signs. Dazed and confused, many people headed toward the front entrances, which were blocked or destroyed, so he directed them to the inner courtyard. As breathing became more difficult from the fumes, smoke, and heat, some people panicked, but his steady voice calmed them.

By now the corridors were filling from floor to ceiling with the thickest, blackest smoke he could imagine. Tarantino ducked into a bathroom, where he snatched paper towels and soaked them. Holding them over his nose and mouth, he charged back into the hallway, but had to crawl on his stomach in order to see below the smoke. Feeling along the wall, he helped assist several workers out to the courtyard.

He did the same thing on the third and second floors before moving to the ground floor, where survivors told him there were more serious injuries farther inside. Ignoring the orders of security personnel to evacuate, Tarantino went against the flow of those fleeing and headed toward the impact area.

The smoke and fumes made him woozy. Worried that he would pass out, he staggered outside onto A&E Drive. After gulping fresh air, he realized he was standing in an area strewn with parts of the plane, including the landing gear, which had punched two holes through the C-Ring wall.

Although he wasn't wearing any protective gear—he was in his summer Navy khaki uniform, slacks and a short-sleeve shirt—Tarantino clutched a fire extinguisher and joined a small group of service people as they fought their way into the breach.

It's not smart to be in here without protection, but I have to go in there, he told himself. *Lives are at stake.*

First there was a deafening roar . . . and then the world turned hot and black for Jerrell "Jerry" Henson. Part of the cockpit and front landing gear of the hijacked plane had plowed through the Navy Command Center on the first floor of the C Ring, triggering a raging firestorm. A huge pile of debris—ceiling tiles, bookcases, wallboard, desks, and plumbing—slammed into the 64-year-old former naval flight officer, pinning his head between his computer monitor and his left shoulder. The rubble would have crushed him had it not been for his desktop. It had landed across the arms of the chair he was sitting in. Although he was trapped, the arms of the chair supported most of the weight of the debris. The chair, however, had collapsed, leaving Henson sitting in an awkward, angled position with his back near the floor. He could move nothing but his left hand and his legs below his knees.

In terrible pain from a head wound that soaked his shoulder in blood, Henson fought to remain conscious as acrid smoke filled the room. He couldn't see anything because it was darker than midnight. Henson could hear two of his staff members, Petty Officers Christine Williams and Charles Lewis, who were injured and covered by debris nearby. With smoke burning their eyes and throats, all three began yelling for help. They didn't get any response as the room continued to burn and melt around them.

From inside the larger hole that led to part of the command center, Thomas heard other people screaming for help behind a metal door. *One of them could be Bob,* he thought. Somebody handed him a four-foot-long iron bar, and he began pounding on the door, trying to break it open. But this was in a high-security area, so the door was sealed with an electric lock and wouldn't give.

Harsh smoke from burning insulation, jet fuel, and paper stung his lungs and set off a coughing fit as he wailed away on the door. But eventually the voices faded. *Did they find another way out . . . or are they dying? I've got to find a new way in.*

Grabbing a fire extinguisher, he crawled into the smaller of the two holes, where the smoke was thicker and the heat hotter. But he had to back out to find better protection. He took off his uniform shirt, because the polyester was beginning to melt. He picked up a discarded towel, wet it, and wrapped it around his bare head to shield it from the radiant heat. Then he dove back in, linking up with service members who were already inside fighting the blaze.

Suddenly, a woman in an army uniform dashed out from the smoke, ran smack into Thomas, and kept on going. *I'm glad to see she got out. Maybe Doles will come out next.*

Thomas, Tarantino, and the other rescuers took turns battling the fire in the command center. One or two at a time would spray their extinguishers for a few minutes, then rotate back out while others would rush in. Together, they pushed farther into the devastated office. Outside, other men took off their T-shirts, soaked them in water, tore them in strips, and passed them inside for the rescuers to wear over their noses.

For ten minutes, Henson and Petty Officers Williams and Lewis were pleading for help. While he was hollering, Henson managed to yank enough debris loose with his left hand to free his head. But he was still pinned at the waist. Fortunately, he could move his legs, so he exercised them to keep them from going to sleep. If he ever got freed, he would need legs primed for escape.

Because he was sucking in bad air, he tried to limit his breathing, but he couldn't hold it in for long. With every breath, the smoke displaced the air in his lungs, creating a feeling of being choked or strangled. He figured that if help didn't arrive, he had about five minutes left to live. Between coughs, he frantically yelled, trying to get someone's attention. But the toxic smoke was burning his throat, causing his voice to get weaker and scratchier.

No longer hearing Williams and Lewis hacking or shouting for help, Henson wondered if they were still alive. The only sounds reaching his ears were the crackling flames, trickling water from broken sprinklers, and snapping live wires.

Thomas and Tarantino were too busy to notice each other in the smoky chaos as they and the other rescuers kept advancing into what was a house of horrors. Melting metal and plastic from the ceiling dripped down on them, searing their arms and head, and burning holes in their T-shirts. Tarantino had already torn off his uniform shirt, fearing that its synthetic fibers would melt and burn his skin.

With the soles of their shoes melting, they ventured deeper into what had been the new command center's super-secret information-gathering room. It was filled with miles of snarled wires, cables, and lines to monitors and communications equipment.

While making a path by throwing aside flaming debris, the men faced exposed live wires that were throwing off sparks and arcing over their heads. Because the rescuers had to step in puddles from leaking pipes and sprinklers, they were getting zapped whenever their bare arms, legs, or head touched one of the wires. The electrical shocks hurt, but were tolerable.

The men, whose hands were bloody and scraped, were also getting pelted by falling tiles and fragments as they crouched to stay below the heat and smoke.

"Doles! Doles! Are you in there?" Thomas shouted. He kept calling out Dolan's name and for anyone else to come toward him.

In another part of the room, Tarantino waved a flashlight that someone had given him.

Hearing Thomas's voice and seeing the flashlight, Williams and Lewis shook off their grogginess, staggered to their feet, and stumbled toward Tarantino.

"We would have died, because we didn't know how to get out," Williams said.

As he directed them to the makeshift exit, Tarantino asked, "Are there other people inside?"

"Yeah, at least one other person."

Henson knew the room was completely sealed, blocked at its entrance by mounds of fiery debris. The increasing rain of melting metal and plastic from the ceiling told him the room couldn't last much longer. Unless there was a hole somewhere for rescuers, he assumed, he was doomed. But he didn't dwell on death.

He had been trained for emergency responses, having flown 72 combat missions during the Vietnam War. On those missions, Henson and his crew had flown through walls of deadly flak from antiaircraft guns. There had been nights when his plane had to land in bad weather on a pitching aircraft carrier and with the fuel gauge on empty.

But in his 40 years of naval service, Henson had never felt so close to death as he did now. He was focused on getting out. Survival trumped every other thought, so he put all his energy into trying to free himself, no matter how futile it seemed. He continued to holler for help, because he didn't have any other option. If somebody didn't help free him, he was going to die.

Thomas worked his way farther in toward Dolan's work space, while Tarantino took a different path deeper into the inferno.

Seeing nothing but flames, Thomas shouted his best buddy's name over and over. "Dolan! Dolan! Where are you?" *If he's in here, there's no way he could still be alive,* Thomas thought. *But I have to keep looking.* He moved to within 30 feet of where he thought Dolan's desk would have been.

"Doles! Doles! Say something!" Thomas yelled. From the flickering light of nearby flames, he caught movement under a pile of debris. He edged closer. *What am I looking at? It's like a jack-o'-lantern turned sideways.* Through the dense smoke, he saw a pair of eyes staring at him. And then they blinked. *It's a man's face! Oh my God, there's a guy in here!*

Thomas started yelling, "Hey, there's a guy in here! I've found someone!"

It was Henson, still in his chair, which was knocked sideways near the floor. He was drifting into unconsciousness. "I don't know if he's still with us or not!" Thomas shouted.

I've got to get him out of here because he's about to catch on fire, Thomas thought. The fit, 6-foot-1, 160-pound captain clambered toward Henson and then tried to lift the debris. Nothing budged. "Help! Help!

There's a guy in here, and he's trapped!" Thomas shouted. *He's going to die, and I'll watch him die if I can't lift this stuff off him.* Thomas shoved his shoulder into the rubble and put his hands underneath it. He braced himself, squatted, and used every ounce of strength he had. Still, it wouldn't move. "Someone come help me!"

It was getting harder to yell, and even tougher to breathe.

Entering from a different part of the devastated command center, Tarantino came across a jumble of burning, uprooted cubicles. Earlier, someone had handed him a wet T-shirt, which he tied around his face for protection—however minimal—against the smoke and powerful fumes.

The severe heat toasted his skin, making it feel as if he had stepped into a blast furnace. Exposed live wires and choking smoke reminded him how much danger he was in. He wished he could turn around and leave, but he felt compelled to push on.

Then he heard Thomas's shouts. Tarantino turned his flashlight toward the voice and from ten feet away spotted Henson, his face bloodied, bruised, and blackened from soot.

I can't believe he's still alive. Tarantino could barely tolerate the heat and the fumes in the few minutes he had been in the room. Yet Henson had been suffering in this torment for at least 15 minutes. Seeing flames spreading on one side of the rubble that was holding down Henson, Tarantino shouted at him, "You've got to move now! You don't have much time!"

"I can't," Henson responded. "I'm stuck. My legs are pinned. I've been trying and trying, but I can't move."

I need him to come to me, Tarantino thought. *I don't think I can go in any farther.*

Although Henson seemed composed, it sounded like the fight was going out of him. He was drifting in and out of consciousness from his injuries and lack of oxygen. *He doesn't have long to live.*

Meanwhile, on the opposite side of the rubble that was imprisoning Henson, Thomas thought, *I can't let this guy die. This just isn't right.* Thomas was still struggling to shift the pile off of Henson.

Just then, frantic voices from outside began yelling, "Get out! Get out! The building's collapsing!"

Tarantino, Thomas, and Henson could feel the room quiver and hear it creak and groan. Several secondary explosions, apparently from the plane's fuel tanks, rocked the building, sending debris falling from the ceiling. The men feared the command center was about to cave in.

Tarantino stared into Henson's eyes and saw fear, but also hope—hope that he would be saved. *We can't leave him,* the doctor thought. *It's us or nobody.* Tarantino got down on his hands and knees and slithered on his belly along popping wires and the smoldering debris until he reached Henson.

"Hey, I'm a flight surgeon, a navy doctor," Tarantino told him. "We're going to get you out of here." Tarantino took off the wet T-shirt he had over his face, gave it to Henson, and said, "Breathe through that."

Tarantino and Thomas started working together without introducing themselves. There was no time. Their unspoken collaboration was natural and instinctive, because that's the way navy people respond when there's a fire on a ship.

Tarantino stood up and tried to pull Henson out from under the debris. He couldn't move him. So he tried to lift the rubble, while Thomas did the same from the other side. They still couldn't dislodge it.

We have to get this guy out now, or all three of us are going to die, Thomas thought. He gave himself a quick pep talk: *Push harder, pull harder, yell louder, make it happen now! We're not leaving without one another. We're not going to die!*

Tarantino was about to pass out from the smoke and fumes. Frustrated and desperate, he thought, *I don't know what else I can do.* But he wouldn't give up. *Think of something fast!* Then he did. The 6-foot-4, 180-pound triathlete had strong legs, having rowed crew for Stanford University. He dropped to the floor, flopped on his back, and put his feet up under the debris that was squishing Henson at the waist. Then, like he had so many times during training in college, Tarantino leg-pressed as hard as he could. Slowly he raised the rubble, first an inch, then two, and finally five inches.

It was just enough room for Henson to start wriggling free.

Thomas, amazed at the doctor's strength, wedged his shoulder underneath the debris to take some of the pressure off Tarantino's legs. Grunting and sweating while his legs held up the rubble, Tarantino used his right arm to clutch Henson.

"Move your butt!" he yelled. "It's now or never! You've got to get out of here right now!"

Tarantino then began pulling him out across his body, warning him, "Don't knock my legs, because I don't want the debris to fall down on us."

Henson grasped Tarantino's arm, then his neck, and pulled himself over the doctor toward Thomas. But his progress was halted. "My foot is stuck on something," he said. "I can't move."

"Get him out!" Tarantino shouted to Thomas. "I can't hold this thing much longer!"

Thomas discovered that Henson's foot was snagged on a cable and quickly untangled it. "Go! Go! Go!" he urged Henson. "Come on, man, you can do it!"

Henson yanked his foot out of his shoe and continued to crawl. Thomas helped him to his feet, put Henson's arm around his shoulder, and dragged him toward the opening.

"Is there anyone else in here?" Tarantino asked Henson.

"Yes," Henson replied. "I think there are others."

I really didn't want to hear that, Tarantino thought.

I need to get out of here right now, too. His legs shaking from strain, Tarantino called out into the smoky darkness, "Is there anyone else in here? Speak up!"

Not hearing anyone, Tarantino began lowering the mass he had been lifting. But now he had a new worry: *Did I unsettle the debris so that I'll end up trapped under it?* Fortunately, he was able to lower it so that he could slip out from underneath. He staggered through the hole into the daylight, coughing and retching.

Craig Powell—the muscular SEAL who moments earlier had helped Colonel Philip McNair's people escape the flames—was at the opening, holding up a sagging portion of the ceiling just long enough for Tarantino, Thomas, and Henson to flee. Seconds after they all got out, the whole section collapsed, sending a rush of smoky hot air out from the hole.

Once he stopped gagging and breathed in fresh air, Tarantino put his uniform shirt back on and dashed over to Henson, who was now in a triage area in the courtyard. Determining that Henson was suffering from smoke inhalation, burns, and lacerations, Tarantino directed his immediate care with oxygen, IV fluids, and bandages.

After taking a breather, Thomas went over to Tarantino and introduced himself. "I'm Dave Thomas."

"I'm Dave Tarantino."

As they shook hands, Thomas thought, *I'm going back in the hole, and I know he will, too. If he doesn't make it out, I need to identify who this brave man is.*

Thomas reached over, gripped Tarantino's nametag on the doctor's shirt, and ripped it off. Then he hustled over to Henson, showed him the nametag, and said, "Remember the name. Tarantino. He's the guy who helped save your life."

As Henson was put in an ambulance, he looked up at Tarantino and murmured, "Thank you." It was too hard to talk, because his airway was damaged from the heat and smoke, and his throat hurt from yelling and coughing.

"You're going to be all right," Tarantino assured him.

Following the military's unwritten code never to leave anyone behind, Tarantino and Thomas hurried toward the hole to see if they could do more. But the heat, flames, and smoke made it impossible to enter. The firefighters who had just arrived couldn't get into the breach, either, even with their protective fire-resistant gear and self-contained breathing apparatuses.

Tarantino stayed in the area, hoping that by some miracle more survivors would emerge. But none did. Henson was the last person in the Pentagon brought out alive.

Thomas's heart weighed heavy over the fate of his closest friend and of all those in the impact area who hadn't been found. He was injured and fatigued—and extremely angered by the suicide attacks. Wrapped in a barbwire of negativity, he needed to think of something else to free himself from this painful gloom. Then it dawned on him. And for one brief moment, he felt jubilant. He had just reminded himself, *We saved a life today.*

Lieutenant Commander David Tarantino and Captain David Thomas suffered smoke inhalation, and cuts and burns on their heads, hands, knees, and feet. Tarantino also sustained a strained knee from his courageous leg-press. But both were back at work the next day at the still-smoldering Pentagon.

For their brave efforts, they were each awarded the Navy and Marine Corps Medal for heroism.

"Their heroism is a step beyond what any medal could recognize," declares Jerry Henson. "I don't have words to describe how brave they were. I was definitely a dead guy if they hadn't come in after me, because there was no way I could get out of there. Tarantino and Thomas didn't have any breathing apparatus or equipment other than some wet T-shirts over their heads and a fire extinguisher that they pulled off the wall. They really had nothing but courage coming in there. Fire was all over. The rubble that they crawled across was unsound. Things were burning them, and with all that, they kept coming because they knew there was a guy in there who was still breathing. It was just an incredible act of bravery.

"I'm eternally grateful, but not surprised. There's never been any doubt in my mind about the quality and responsiveness of the American sailor—an absolutely incredible individual."

Henson spent four days in the hospital, where he was

treated for smoke damage to the lining of his throat and lungs, and lacerations on his head, ear, and chin. A week after his release, he thanked Tarantino and Thomas when they visited him and his family.

"It was such a rewarding feeling to hear their gratitude," Tarantino recalls.

Adds Thomas, "Seeing Jerry and Dave was a ray of sunshine piercing through the darkness, because of all the casualties at the Pentagon. Jerry's a great guy, a wonderful man. He and his family reaffirmed the good in the world."

Twenty-eight of the dead had worked in the Navy Command Center—and among the casualties was Thomas's best friend, Captain Robert Dolan. Recovered with his remains was his Naval Academy class ring. Captain Dolan was buried at sea in a ceremony attended by Thomas.

"I think about him every day," says Thomas. "There wasn't a day for a long time that I didn't cry whenever I thought of him. The true heroes are people like Bob's wife, Lisa, who picked up the pieces and carried on, raised their two kids, and kept his memory alive. He was a great naval officer, an even better man, father, husband, and friend."

Since 9/11, Thomas has served as the deputy chief of staff for Global Force Management and Joint Operations on the staff of commander, U.S. Fleet Forces Command; commander, Joint Task Force, Guantanamo Bay, Cuba; commander, Carrier Strike Group Two; and commander, Naval Surface Force Atlantic.

Promoted to rear admiral, Thomas has been awarded the Defense Superior Service Medal, the Legion of Merit, and the Bronze Star.

After 9/11, Tarantino coordinated humanitarian efforts in Iraq and Afghanistan and earned a Bronze Star. He was an adviser to the Iraqi ministry of health and worked on international health issues for the military at the Pentagon. He earned a masters degree in public health and was awarded a fellowship in preventive medicine. Promoted to commander, he became director of preventive medicine and public health for the Marines in the Pacific region.

In 2003, the American Medical Association awarded him its Medal of Valor. He accepted the award on behalf of those lost on September 11.

"As a physician and navy medical officer, I'm trained to go into harm's way and not leave anyone behind," he says. "There are core values of honor, courage, and commitment that we try to live up to. That's all I was trying to do."

Tarantino threw away his damaged uniform and even tossed out his shoes; the soles had melted. But Thomas kept his ruined khakis—as well as Tarantino's nametag—as a reminder of that infamous day.

When the Smithsonian National Museum of American History began collecting objects to document the 9/11 attacks, Thomas donated his uniform and Tarantino's nametag to its exhibit September 11: Bearing Witness to History. *You can view all the objects online at http://americanhistory.si.edu/september11/.*

"Follow My Voice!
I Know a Way Out!"

LIEUTENANT COLONEL VICTOR CORREA
United States Army

The billowing dense smoke was burning his eyes, throat, and lungs. He couldn't see, and he could hardly breathe. The intense heat felt as though his skin was ready to blister. But Lieutenant Colonel Victor Correa wasn't ready to flee the blazing Pentagon office area—not when he knew there were coworkers inside, not when he knew there was an escape route for them.

But many of his civilian colleagues were too scared to move. Some were huddled under their desks. Others were screaming or crying in panic. And there were those who were confused and disoriented, crawling to nowhere, lost in a nightmare of fire and fumes, falling ceiling tiles, and sparking live wires.

Correa had only seconds to command their attention and gain their confidence. In a manner he hoped was strong and convincing, he hollered into the blackness, "If you can hear my voice, come toward me! I can lead you out! There's a way out of here! I can help you!"

They would have to run through the smoke and flames toward a voice coming from someone they couldn't see. He waited and wondered, *Will they come? Will they believe me?* Time was running out before the flames and smoke would kill him and anyone still in the newly renovated wedge of the Pentagon. Fighting back the urge to gag from the acrid smoke, he bellowed again, "Hurry and follow my voice!"

Minutes earlier, Correa, who worked as a recruiting policy analyst for the Army Reserve and National Guard, was in a second-floor office in the E Ring watching replays on TV of the jetliners smashing into the Twin Towers. Disgusted by what he saw, he went back to his desk to talk about it with his colleague, Major John Jessup.

"You know, sir, this could happen here," Jessup said. "We're as vulnerable as the towers. The terrorists could strike us. . . ."

KA-BOOM! A thundering explosion rocked the Pentagon, flinging a shock wave that threw Jessup against nearby lockers and sent Correa flying ten feet in the air. While he was still airborne, his mind captured the terror in slow motion. Seeing a big ball of fire rocketing toward him, he ducked and looked away toward the office's blast-proof windows. Like inflated balloons, they bowed out from the concussive force before returning to their regular shape. He landed hard on his hip. Before he had a chance to absorb what was happening, the floor began shaking violently.

He didn't know that the hijacked American Airlines Flight 77 had just crashed into the west side of the Pentagon and was careening through the first-floor offices directly below him, knocking out support columns. Every time a column collapsed, it sounded like an explosion and opened a hole or crack on the floor of the second story, allowing flames to shoot up.

Although he had been in the army for most of his adult life, Correa had never experienced combat. It didn't matter. He automatically followed his military training: Assess the situation, gather as much information as you can, then take action either as a leader or a follower. His inner voice told him, *You're okay, but there are people who need your help, so get up and start helping.* That's when he sprang to his feet.

As smoke began filling the large office area, he could see that many people were so shocked they were rooted to their desks or standing still. They didn't know what to do or where to go.

He hustled over to Jessup and told him, "We're going to get people out of here." Pointing to an exit about 30 yards away, Correa said, "I'm going to send people to you, and you're going to guide them out."

The work area was almost entirely shrouded in black from the smoke, and although he couldn't see the flames nearby, he certainly could feel them. "If you can hear my voice, come toward me because I know a way out of here!" he shouted over and over. Workers started emerging from the smoke, some still in emotional shock. Correa grabbed them and hustled them over to Jessup. "Make sure they get out, and then come back and get more," Correa said. "I'll stay here."

Two cubicles away, he saw a civilian worker crawling aimlessly on the floor, so Correa reached down and picked him up. Correa was startled to feel the man's back—it was scorching hot. He guided him over to Jessup, who shepherded him and others safely away.

The thick smoke was sinking to waist level, forcing Correa to crouch. He kept yelling for people to come to his voice, which was getting hoarser by the second.

By now the heat and smoke were nearly intolerable. "John, you've got to leave now," he told Jessup. "Make sure those you helped out of here are okay."

"I want to stay here with you until everybody's out. Besides, you need someone to cover your back."

"Don't worry about me," said Correa. "I'll be all right."

After Jessup left reluctantly, Correa checked one more time to make sure nobody was left behind. "Listen to my voice!" he rasped. "Focus on the sound of my voice! Hurry!"

From out of the smoky darkness, more coworkers staggered forward. "Go down the corridor and make a quick right," he directed them. "There's an exit, and you'll see the light from a window. It will lead you to safety. Go!"

He was now on his hands and knees to stay under the smoke. Even though it was getting increasingly difficult for him to breathe, he kept calling out for any other people to come forward. He waited for as long as he dared. Finally the flames and smoke forced him to back out into the corridor. *I hope everyone got out. God, I hope they got out.*

Correa then spotted Lieutenant Colonel Brian Birdwell writhing on the floor of Corridor 4. When the plane had struck the Pentagon, Birdwell was knocked off his feet and engulfed in flames. Now he was in agony, his clothes smoldering. Rushing over to help, Correa joined Colonel Karl Knoblauch, Lieutenant Colonel George Richon, and Captain Lance Giddens. When they reached Birdwell, he was so badly burned that they couldn't pick him up because they knew his skin would come off.

"Let's make a hammock with our arms," suggested Knoblauch. The four officers stood across from each other, extended their arms, crossed them, and clasped hands to form a human hammock. Then they told Birdwell to fall back and lie on their arms, which he did. As they carried him down the corridor, they could feel the heat from his body through what was left of his burnt clothes.

On their way out, their exit was blocked by a fire door that was designed to automatically close off the corridor to prevent the spread of smoke and flames. Correa pulled and yanked on the door, but it wouldn't open. "How are we going to get out of here?" he asked.

"Come on, I know another way out," Richon said. They carried Birdwell to Corridor 5, only to happen upon another fire door. But this one had been jammed open, allowing them to get past it to the courtyard, where medics were waiting to treat casualties.

Worried that others would be trapped behind the fire door in Corridor 4, Correa dashed back into the burning Pentagon to the safe side of that fire door. He heard people on the other side gasping for air, screaming for help, crying, and praying.

With all his might and muscle, Correa tried to pry open the fire door, but it wouldn't budge. "Don't give up!" he shouted. His words were meant not only for those on the other side, but for himself as well. He continued to tug and jerk at the door.

"Please get us out of here!" someone shouted. "The smoke is getting worse! We can't breathe!" Others pounded on the door, begging to be freed.

"Don't give up!" he yelled again. *I've got to get this door open or they'll die.*

Just then, Colonel Knoblauch and Sergeant Major Tony Rose appeared. Together, the three used brute force to shove open the door just wide enough for people to squeeze through. As smoke poured out, the trapped workers streamed forward, some stopping just long enough to thank Correa and the others.

Two workers agreed to stay at the fire door to keep it

open. Because that allowed some of the smoke to escape, Correa, Knoblauch, and Rose went back inside, searching for survivors who were still trapped or didn't know how to escape.

It was getting so difficult to breathe that Correa and the others took off their shirts, soaked them in water from a drinking fountain, and wrapped them around their nose and mouth, but that didn't help much. They decided it was better putting on their shirts, which offered some protection from falling debris and hot ashes.

They spread out in the smoky, fire-riddled office area and moved forward as far as they could and yelled. Then they ran out to inhale slightly better air before rushing back in and shouting for people to come to them.

"Follow my voice! I know the way out of here!" Correa croaked in the darkness, coughing badly between words.

Just when it seemed too hot and too smoky for anyone to survive, several more people stumbled out from behind the flames. "We had just said our last prayers," wheezed one woman. "We were trapped and didn't know where to go. Thank you!"

Somewhere inside, Carl Mahnken, a civilian in the Army public affairs office, was lying unconscious. When the jetliner had plowed into the Pentagon, the floor under him had cracked open, causing flames to shoot up. As he jumped away, he had fallen backward and been knocked out.

Mahnken was drawn back to consciousness by

Correa's constant shouting of "Follow my voice! I know a way out!" Mahnken lurched to his feet and dragged himself through the smoke and fire toward Correa's voice.

"I was knocked out, and then I could hear your voice over and over," Mahnken told him. "It sounded far, far away. But that's what stimulated me to wake up. Your voice made me come back to consciousness. Thank you."

Convinced there was no one left alive in that particular area, Correa and the others hustled outside onto A&E Drive, where they saw Colonel Philip McNair and his colleagues at the Army personnel office clumped around an opening in the frame of a second-floor window. Some were afraid to jump, so Correa, Knoblauch, and Rose sprinted over to a nearby Dumpster and shoved it under the window. That allowed other rescuers to set up a ladder that reached the second floor.

After they left the building, Correa borrowed a cell phone and got through to his wife, Oretta, who was seven months pregnant with their third child. "Don't talk, just listen," he told her. "I'm okay. Not to worry." He could hear her crying. "There's a lot to be done here," he said. "I'll get home when I finish my job. I've got to go now. I love you." He hung up without giving her a chance to talk.

He and his comrades joined another group of rescuers hoping to find survivors in the fiery C Ring. But the flames were too powerful and drove them back out, so they assisted the firefighters any way they could. Correa and the others were now resigned to the harsh reality that there would be no more rescue attempts.

Late in the afternoon, a general came over to Correa and told him, "Time for you to go home."

Correa wasn't ready to leave without first walking around part of the Pentagon's perimeter to survey the damage. He was stunned by the destruction to the west side of what most everyone believed was the world's most secure building. *The terrorists attacked us on our own soil! And they killed so many innocent people, coworkers and friends I'll never see again.* The thought made him sick to his stomach.

Although he was exhausted, he chose to walk home, which was only ten minutes from the Pentagon. When he stepped into his house, Oretta gasped. His uniform was ruined by burn marks, ash, and blood, and it smelled of jet fuel. Correa's face was covered in soot. She came running toward him, but he held up his hand. He didn't want her to hug him until he was cleaned up. "Tell everyone I'm fine," he said. "I need to take a shower."

He went into the bedroom, stripped off his uniform, and walked toward the shower. Suddenly, he felt a sharp pain in his hip and collapsed to the floor. He hadn't realized until then that he had injured his hip when he was thrown through the air by the initial blast. The adrenaline racing through his body had blocked the pain. But now that he wasn't in any danger, his body had stopped pumping adrenaline. He crawled to his bed and pulled himself up and lay there until the pain subsided. Then he took a shower. Alone with his thoughts, he relived the events of the day: the explosion, the fire, the smoke, the screams, the panic, the rescues, the deaths. It was all too much to bear. He broke down and wept, wishing that the shower spray could wash away the feeling of despair.

When he regained his composure, he stepped out of the shower and put on a clean uniform. Then, despite the pain in his hip, he walked back to the Pentagon, where he joined several surviving colleagues who also felt a need to return to the scene of the attack. They sat under trees and tried to cope by sharing their fears, their heartache, their brushes with death.

The next morning, the pain Correa felt was so excruciating that he went to Fort Belvoir Hospital, where he was treated for a dislocated hip. Doctors also discovered that his lungs were harmed from inhaling smoke and fumes from jet fuel, which were triggering coughing jags.

He left the hospital later that day and went to work at the temporary offices set up in Rosslyn, Virginia. As he explained to Oretta, "It's important for me to go back to work, because otherwise I'll have given the enemy a moral victory. They hit us hard, but they didn't knock us out."

As bad as September 11 was, in some ways the next day was worse for the Pentagon survivors. They learned that 125 fellow service members and civilian workers were confirmed dead or missing—and every one knew that, in this case, *missing* meant "dead."

The death toll made Correa wonder, *Was there more that I could have done? Were there more people I could have saved?* But over the next few days, Pentagon workers came up to him to thank him for being the vocal beacon that led them to safety.

As Lieutenant Colonel Phil Smith told him, "You were the one who was yelling, and that helped me find my way out. Because of you, I am alive today."

For his heroism on September 11, Victor Correa was awarded the Soldier's Medal for valor and the Purple Heart for his injuries. He later was promoted to colonel.

Even though Lieutenant Colonel Brian Birdwell suffered serious burns over 60 percent of his body, he survived. Birdwell, who retired from the army, underwent 39 operations to rebuild his body. He has repeatedly told the media how grateful he is that his rescuers had the strength and fortitude to save him from certain death.

Says Correa, "We [rescuers] were conscious of the danger we faced, but we had an overwhelming feeling to save as many lives as possible. It was our duty, obligation, and desire as humans to help those in need."

He credits his military training with reacting swiftly and confidently in the minutes after the Pentagon was attacked. "I was taught to always be prepared for the unexpected and to remain calm under pressure," he says. "That's what I tried to do."

After serving 22 years in the army, Correa retired and moved to South Carolina, where he spends time with his wife, Oretta, and their five children. The 9/11 attack on the Pentagon, though, is never far from his mind. "I still get nightmares," he admits. "I don't like crowded or enclosed places, and I always want to be outdoors. I avoid being too close to friends, because I had so many torn away from me."

Correa says he keeps a scrapbook of that day for posterity, but downplays his role as a hero. "The word hero belongs to the firefighters who died at the World Trade Center and the passengers who fought the hijackers on the plane that went down in Pennsylvania. They are the heroes who paid the ultimate price."

UNITED FLIGHT 93

No one will ever know exactly what happened on doomed United Flight 93 after four terrorists hijacked the jetliner on the morning of September 11. What is known is that the hijackers failed in their suicide mission to wreak death and destruction in our nation's capital. They failed solely because the courageous passengers and crew rose up against them in a spontaneous rebellion that ended when the plane crashed in a field, killing all on board. Based on the findings in the 9/11 Commission Report, transcripts of the cockpit voice recorder and radio transmissions, and published interviews with family and friends of passengers who made last-minute calls from the plane, here is the incredible story of these heroic passengers.

United Flight 93

Newark, NJ
Shanksville, PA
Washington, D.C.

"Okay, Let's Roll!"

PASSENGERS AND CREW
United Flight 93

When United Flight 93 took off from Newark, New Jersey, at 8:42 A.M. on September 11, only four of the 44 people on board knew everyone would soon die.

The four were Islamic fanatics who had trained for two years to hijack this plane and crash it into one of America's greatest symbols of democracy and freedom—either the White House or the Capitol building in Washington, D.C.

About 45 minutes after takeoff, the terrorists began carrying out their deadly plot with cold-blooded efficiency. Their plane was one of four jetliners hijacked by their fellow suicidal extremists that morning. The other three planes had already struck their targets. Everything would have gone according to plan had the hijackers on Flight 93 not made one crucial mistake. They failed to consider that the crew and passengers—common, everyday people who loved their families and their country—would revolt and willingly sacrifice their lives to thwart the evil scheme.

Because of heavy air traffic, the Boeing 757 had left Newark International Airport 41 minutes late, bound for San Francisco. Besides the four terrorists, the wide-body twin-engine aircraft carried two pilots, five flight attendants, and only 33 passengers. Early in the flight, salespersons, professionals, retirees, students, executives, and others chose to read, sleep, or eat breakfast. Most were flying for business reasons. But some were heading home after family gatherings—Rich Guadagno had celebrated the 100th birthday of his grandmother, while Lauren Grandcolas had attended her grandmother's funeral. Some were going to California for a vacation, such as 69-year-old Patricia Cushing, who was taking her first commercial flight; and Donald and Jean Peterson who, that very morning, had changed their later flight to this earlier one so they could get to Yosemite National Park sooner.

Captain Jason Dahl, 43, who had learned to fly before he learned to drive, was at the controls. The only reason the Denver-based pilot was flying this particular flight was because he had changed his schedule so he would get time off to take his wife to London to celebrate their anniversary.

As the plane climbed to 35,000 feet over western

Pennsylvania in crystal clear skies, it seemed like a routine flight, which was just the way Dahl and First Officer LeRoy Homer, 36, wanted it. But then at 9:24 A.M., they received a text message from a United flight dispatcher that warned, "Beware any cockpit intrusion—two a/c [aircraft] hit World Trade Center."

Sitting in the first-class section were four Middle Eastern passengers: Lebanese-born Ziad Samir Jarrah, 25; and Saudi Arabians Saeed al-Ghamdi, 21; Ahmed al-Nami, 23; and Ahmed al-Haznawi, 20. They had undergone two years of intense fundamentalist religious instruction, trained in close-quarters combat, lifted weights, and took flying lessons. Jarrah, the leader of the group, went to an American flight school so he could learn to fly the 757.

And now the moment they had prepared for—and longed for—had arrived.

At 9:28 A.M., above eastern Ohio, all four tied red bandannas around their heads and leaped from their seats. First-class passenger Mark "Mickey" Rothenberg, a businessman from Scotch Plains, New Jersey, rose from his seat in 5B, possibly to halt one of the hijackers. He was stabbed in the chest. One of the hijackers grabbed veteran flight attendant Debbie Welsh, 49, and held a box cutter to her throat while the others battered the locked cockpit door.

United 93 suddenly dropped 700 feet. Eleven seconds into the descent, the FAA's air traffic control center in Cleveland received the first of two radio transmissions from the aircraft. "Mayday! Mayday!" yelled Captain Dahl amid the sounds of a violent scuffle in the cockpit. After 35 seconds of silence, he keyed the microphone again. Cleveland air control heard more fighting and shouts of, "Hey get out of here! Get out of here! Get out of here!"

Within four minutes, the pilots had been slashed and left bleeding to death on the floor outside the cockpit. Welsh, who had been on this flight only because she had swapped shifts with another flight attendant, was struggling against her knife-wielding captor. "Don't, don't," she pleaded. "Please, I don't want to die." But when she fought back, her throat was slit.

Jarrah took over the controls. When he jumped into the pilot's seat, he accidentally knocked the plane off autopilot. That caused the aircraft to rise and fall several hundred feet like a roller coaster. After he managed to straighten out the plane, the hijackers, speaking in Arabic, reassured one another: "Everything is fine."

Jarrah got on the intercom and in a thick accent told the shocked passengers: "Ladies and gentlemen: Hear the captain. Please sit down. Keep remaining [sic] sitting. We have a bomb on board. So sit." He wasn't aware that the announcement was also heard by Cleveland air control, because the communication switch was left on. Once he discovered his mistake, the hijackers fiddled with buttons and knobs until they were no longer transmitting.

Stunned by what he was seeing, Tom Burnett, 38, an

executive of a medical-device company, whipped out his cell phone and called his wife, Deena, who was preparing breakfast for their three girls at their home in San Ramon, California.

Hearing Tom's strained voice, she asked him, "Are you okay?"

"No," he replied in a whisper. "I'm on a plane. It's United Flight 93, and we've been hijacked. They've already knifed a guy, and there's a bomb on board. Please call the authorities." Then he hung up.

With two hijackers in the cockpit, the other two guarded the passengers. Some were herded toward the back of the plane to rows 30 through 34. Ahmed al-Haznawi had a red box strapped around his waist that he claimed was a bomb. Some of the passengers weren't convinced it was real. In fact, they made fun of him, although not to his face. To their surprise, he didn't stop them from using their cell phones or the Airfones attached to the seatbacks.

The passengers and flight attendants began making calls, 23 from the seat-back phones alone from 9:31 to 9:53 A.M. Others shared their cell phones with people who had been strangers just minutes before. Some of the calls were short—no more than a few rushed words expressing fear or love. Others, though, talked of defiance. Despite the life-or-death situation they faced, most of the passengers spoke in a calm but tense manner.

They began hatching plans for a revolt. The bigger guys were convinced they could overpower the hijackers. Six-foot-five Mark Bingham, 31, a public relations executive from San Francisco, had played on a national championship rugby team for the University of California–Berkeley. At 6 feet, 220 pounds, Jeremy Glick, 31, of West Milford, New Jersey, was a former national college judo champion. Rich Guadagno, 38, an enforcement officer with the U.S. Fish and Wildlife Service in Eureka, California, had been trained in hand-to-hand combat. William Cashman, 57, of North Bergen, New Jersey, was a retired iron worker and former paratrooper with the 101st Airborne, who knew karate. Linda Gronlund, 46, an automotive executive and outdoorswoman, had a brown belt in karate. Flight attendant CeeCee Lyles, 33, of Fort Myers, Florida, had been a detective on the Fort Pierce (Florida) Police Department. Todd Beamer, 32, an account manager in Cranbury, New Jersey, was an athlete in high school and college. Lou Nacke, 42, a toy-industry executive from New Hope, Pennsylvania, was a weightlifter. There was even a licensed pilot among them: Don Greene, 52, the vice president of a White Plains, New York, company that made safety devices for airlines. With the right instructions from air-traffic controllers, he felt confident he could land the highly automated Boeing 757.

Meanwhile, in San Ramon, Deena Burnett was on the phone with an FBI agent when Tom called again. She clicked over.

"They're in the cockpit now," he said. "The guy they knifed is dead. I tried to help him but I couldn't get a pulse."

Deena told Tom that two hijacked planes had struck the World Trade Center. He relayed the news to the passengers next to him. "Oh my God," he said. "It's a suicide mission."

He began pumping her for information about the attacks, interrupting her from time to time to tell the others nearby what she was saying. Then he hung up.

At 9:35 A.M., as the plane neared Cleveland, it defied the flight plan by making a U-turn and heading east. The hijackers tuned a cockpit radio to the frequency of a navigation beacon at Washington's Ronald Reagan National Airport, just across the Potomac River from the White House and the Capitol, erasing any doubt about their intended destination.

Jarrah came back on the intercom at 9:39 A.M. and said, "Hi, this is the captain. We'd like you all to remain seated. There is a bomb on board. We are going to turn back to the airport. And they have our demands, so please be quiet."

Passenger Jeremy Glick, a sales manager for an Internet company, called his wife, Lyzbeth, in Windham, New York, where she had taken their 11-week-old daughter, Emerson, to visit her parents. Lyzbeth was watching the Twin Towers burning on television as she spoke to him.

Hearing the panic in Lyzbeth's voice, he tried calming her by telling her how much he loved her. Then he began peppering her with questions about the attacks in New York. "Do you think that's where this plane is going to go?" he wondered.

"I doubt it. There's really nothing left to crash into."

"I can't believe this is happening to me." Then he told Lyzbeth how important it was for her and Emerson to be happy, and that he would respect any decisions she had to make in the future.

He told her there were at least three other passengers as big as him, and they were thinking about jumping the hijacker with the alleged bomb and taking back the plane. "What do you think I should do?" he asked.

"You need to do it," she replied.

"Well, I have my butter knife from breakfast," he joked. "Okay, I'm going to put the phone down. I'll be right back. I love you."

Passenger Mark Bingham phoned his mother, Alice Ann Hoglan, a United flight attendant, in California. "Mom, this is Mark Bingham," he said, so flustered that he used his last name. "I just want you to know that I love you." He went on to explain about the hijacking. There was a long pause as if he had put the phone down. Hoglan could hear muffled voices, and then the phone went dead.

Seeing on TV what had happened in New York, Hoglan called Bingham's cell phone and left a message: "Mark, this is your mom. Those terrorists on board probably intend to use your plane as a weapon. Sweetie, you need to do whatever you can to try to stop them. Good luck, sweetie."

At 9:45 A.M., Tom Burnett called his wife, Deena, for the third time. She had been sobbing because she saw that a jetliner had slammed into the Pentagon and assumed it was his plane. "Tom, you're okay!" she gushed, thinking he had somehow survived the crash.

"No, I'm not," he replied.

She told him about the attack on the Pentagon, news which he shared with the passengers around him. Deena could hear them gasp in surprise and shock.

"I'm putting a plan together," he told Deena. "We're going to take back the plane."

"Who's helping you?"

"Different people, several people," he replied. "There's a group of us. Don't worry. We're going to do something. I'll call you back." He hung up.

Sensing the passengers were poised to launch an uprising, the two hijackers in the cabin rushed to the cockpit door and pounded on it, demanding to be let inside so they could hole up there. Jarrah told his fellow terrorist who was acting as copilot, "Let the guys in now." After the four locked themselves in the cockpit, one of them began praying. Another suggested using the ax that hung on the cockpit's back wall to scare the passengers into submission.

United flight attendant Sandy Bradshaw called her husband, Phil, a pilot in Greensboro, North Carolina. "Have you heard what happened?" she said. "Have you heard? We've been hijacked!"

As her astounded husband listened in silence, she

said she was calling from the coach-class galley in the rear of the plane. She told him a group of passengers were putting together a plan to recapture control of the plane. She and two other flight attendants were filling coffeepots with boiling water to throw at the hijackers.

At 9:54 A.M., Burnett called his wife Deena for the fourth time. "Is there anything new?" he asked her.

"No, no reports of any more attacks."

After the two talked about their kids, Burnett said, "We're waiting until we're over a rural area. We're going to take back the airplane."

"No, no, Tom. Just sit down, be still, be quiet, and don't draw attention to yourself."

"No, Deena. If they're going to crash this plane into a building, we're going to have to do something."

"What about the authorities?"

"We can't wait for the authorities. I don't know what they can do, anyway. It's up to us. I think we can do it."

"What can I do?"

"Pray, Deena, just pray."

"I am praying. I love you."

"Don't worry. We're going to do something." Then he hung up.

Passenger Todd Beamer was trying to call his wife, Lisa, but couldn't get through. He pressed "0" on an Airfone and reached Lisa Jefferson, a customer-service supervisor in Oak Brook, Illinois. For 13 minutes, Beamer told Jefferson everything he could about the hijacking so she could pass it on to authorities: four hijackers, two with knives; six passengers in first class, twenty-seven in coach; five flight attendants; no children that he could see.

Beamer, who was seated near the back of the plane, said the pilot and copilot were lying on the floor in first class and appeared to be dead. He told Jefferson that he had two sons, David and Andrew, and that his wife was expecting their third child in January. "If I don't make it, will you please call my wife and let her know how much I love her and my kids?"

"I promise I will," Jefferson replied.

At his request, she joined him in reciting the Lord's Prayer. Then he whispered, "A few of us have decided to jump the guy with the bomb and get back control of the plane."

"Are you sure that's what you want to do?"

"We don't have much choice at this point. I'm going on faith, and that's what I'm going to do." He set the phone down but kept the line open. Then he said to those around him, "Are you guys ready?" Someone answered yes. And then Beamer said, "Okay, let's roll."

It was 9:57 A.M. The passengers stormed the cockpit, using a food cart as a battering ram. Several passengers abruptly ended phone calls with loved ones in order to join the revolt. After talking to her husband for nearly ten minutes, flight attendant Sandy Bradshaw told him, "Everyone's running up to first class. I've got to go. Bye."

Jarrah, the hijacker pilot, began banking the plane

hard to the left and hard to the right, trying to knock the attacking passengers off balance.

At 9:59 A.M., Jarrah told a fellow hijacker in the cockpit to keep blocking the door. Jarrah continued to bank the airplane sharply left and right, but the assault continued. A minute later, he changed tactics and pitched the nose of the aircraft up and down in a bid to throw off the passengers. The cockpit voice recorder captured the sounds of loud thumps, crashes, shouts, and breaking glass and plates.

Jarrah asked his fellow terrorists, "Is that it? Shall we finish it off?"

A hijacker responded, "No. Not yet. When they all come, we finish it off."

The sounds of fighting continued outside the cockpit. Again, Jarrah pitched the nose of the aircraft up and down. Outside the cockpit door, a passenger hollered, "In the cockpit! If we don't, we'll die!"

Sixteen seconds later, a passenger yelled, "Roll it!"

At 10:01 A.M., after two minutes of making the plane bob and lurch, Jarrah stopped the violent maneuvers and bellowed in Arabic, "Allah is the greatest! Allah is the greatest!" He then asked another hijacker, "Is that it? I mean, shall we put it down?"

"Yes, pull it down."

As the passengers continued their attack, a hijacker urged Jarrah, "Pull it down! Pull it down!"

Although the hijackers remained at the controls, they knew the passengers were only seconds from breaking into the cockpit and overpowering them. As the airplane streaked earthward, Jarrah turned it hard to the right, causing the jetliner to roll on its back in a death spiral. The hijackers began shouting, "Allah is the greatest! Allah is the greatest!"

Flight attendant CeeCee Lyles had been talking to her husband, Lorne, on the phone and cried, "Aah, it feels like the plane's going down!" Referring to the passenger revolt, she said, "They're forcing their way into the cockpit!" Moments later, she screamed, "They're doing it! They're doing it! They're doing it!"

Her husband heard shouting in the background followed by loud whooshing and more shrieking. Lisa Jefferson, still listening to the phone that Todd Beamer had lain down, heard those same sounds along with women screaming, "Oh my God!" and "God help us!" Mixed in were the noises of the raid on the cockpit and then . . . sudden silence.

It was 10:03 A.M. when the jetliner plowed nose first at 580 miles per hour into an empty field in Shanksville, Pennsylvania, 80 miles southeast of Pittsburgh. The impact killed all on board, leaving a large charred crater littered with small pieces of debris no bigger than a telephone book. The plane was only 20 minutes flying time away from the terrorists' intended target in Washington, D.C.

Despite all the painstaking planning and years of rigorous training, the hijackers had failed to hit a national landmark or strike a populated area. They were defeated by a courageous bunch of unarmed passengers and crew who, at the cost of their lives, banded together within minutes to prevent a disaster at the center of American government.

The hijackers were stopped by the heroes of United Flight 93.

While the nation reeled from the September 11 attacks, Americans gained strength and courage from the selfless actions of the passengers and crew of Flight 93 in the face of adversity and death. The crash site quickly turned into a place of spur-of-the-moment gatherings where people from all walks of life came to pay tribute to the heroes.

Following an exhaustive government field investigation and recovery effort during the fall of 2001, the crater was backfilled and the area was fenced off and planted with grass and wildflowers. Local leaders, families of the passengers and crew, and the National Park Service worked together to create the Flight 93 National Memorial at what was once a common field, but is now a field of honor.

The park is dedicated to the heroism, bravery, and sacrifice of the passengers and crew. It is also designed to celebrate their lives. As its mission statement says, "May all who visit this place remember the collective acts of courage and sacrifice of the passengers and crew, revere this hallowed ground as the final resting place of those heroes, and reflect on the power of individuals who choose to make a difference."

About the Author

Allan Zullo is the author of more than 100 nonfiction books on subjects ranging from sports and the supernatural to history and animals.

He has introduced Scholastic readers to the Ten True Tales series, gripping stories of extraordinary persons—many of them young people—who have met the challenges of dangerous, sometimes life-threatening, situations. Among the books in the series are *War Heroes: Voices from Iraq, Battle Heroes: Voices from Afghanistan,* and *World War II Heroes.* In addition, he has authored three books about the real-life experiences of kids during the Holocaust—*Survivors: True Stories of Children in the Holocaust, Heroes of the Holocaust: True Stories of Rescues by Teens,* and *Escape: Children of the Holocaust.*

Allan, a grandfather of five and the father of two grown daughters, lives with his wife, Kathryn, on the side of a mountain near Asheville, North Carolina. To learn more about the author, visit his website at www.allanzullo.com.